Beginner's Guide to
WOODTURNING

By the same author

The Manual of Woodturning

Beginner's Guide to WOODTURNING

REVISED EDITION

Gordon Stokes

PELHAM BOOKS
Stephen Greene Press

PELHAM BOOKS/Stephen Greene Press

Published by the Penguin Group
27 Wrights Lane, London W8 5TZ, England
Viking Penguin Inc., 40 West 23rd Street, New
York, New York 10010, USA
The Stephen Greene Press Inc., 15 Muzzey Street,
Lexington, Massachusetts 02173, USA
Penguin Books Australia Ltd, Ringwood,
Victoria, Australia
Penguin Books Canada Ltd, 2801 John Street,
Markham, Ontario, Canada L3R 1B4
Penguin Books (NZ) Ltd, 182-190 Wairau Road,
Auckland 10, New Zealand

Penguin Books Ltd, Registered Offices:
Harmondsworth, Middlesex, England

First published 1974
Reprinted 1976 (twice), 1979 and 1982
Revised edition published 1985 — Reprinted 1990

Typeset, printed and bound by
Butler & Tanner Ltd, Frome

A CIP catalogue record for this book is available
from the British Library.

ISBN 0 7207 1630 6

Contents

Introduction

This is my forty fifth year in the craft of woodturning, and for the past twenty of those years I have been engaged in running short courses of instruction, for small groups of people, in my own workshops. This is the ideal way to approach the craft, since the combination of lecture, demonstration, and practical 'hands-on' experience combines to cover thoroughly the vital aspects of safety and efficiency. I take a maximum of three students on a course, so that the instruction remains on an individual basis, and have now taught more than three thousand students, many of whom have gone on to build up small businesses and some even to teach the subject. Most of my students have never touched a turning tool before coming to me, and many have never seen wood being turned. They arrive from all parts of the British Isles and from most overseas countries, and they leave with sufficient basic knowledge of the tools, equipment, and techniques to enable them to progress rapidly and safely through practice.

Much of my time has also been spent in demonstrating at the major shows and exhibitions, both here and overseas, which has provided an opportunity for me to discuss the problems of beginners with a very large number of men and women. I feel that experience of this nature is indispensable to anyone wishing to instruct successfully in the craft. The fact is that the same questions crop up whenever I appear in public, and this has placed me in a very strong position from which to evaluate the difficulties which must be overcome by newcomers to the woodturning lathe.

Unfortunately, it is not easy to be certain of obtaining satisfactory instruction in this craft, and a poor standard of instruction can be worse than none at all. The problem here, as the old saying has it, is that 'in the country of the blind, the one-eyed man is king' – so it is not always a good idea to emulate the local woodturner, who may well be doing things very badly. The expenditure of a reasonable sum of money on good tuition, from someone who has been established for a fair number of years, will be a good investment. It may well save a beginner from injury, and will certainly reduce the frustration which goes with bad techniques. Beginners should not be put off by the inevitable awkwardness of things in the early stages, for if there was no challenge, the attempt would hardly be worthwhile.

Those who already have some knowledge of the craft will, I hope, find points in this book which are interesting and helpful, but my major concern is with the real beginner, on whose part I cannot afford to assume any prior knowledge.

My own introduction to woodturning

came at the age of fifteen, when I was presented with a small treadle-operated lathe. I was quite unable to leave the wretched thing alone, but I had no glimmering of an idea at that time where my addiction was to lead me. That was in 1944, a long time ago, and I am sure that the tools and techniques I tried to employ then were very far from being correct. Many a perfectly good piece of timber must have been sacrificed in the name of research, and without a doubt I must have made every mistake in the book. All this, while providing valuable experience, meant that I took a long time over making progress, and was lucky not to injure myself. Nowadays I try hard to put myself in the place of my students, and the readers of my books and articles, so that I am better able to offer advice which will facilitate the gradual build-up of confidence on a firm footing of fundamental understanding.

Confidence is very important, and the right amount of it is a godsend, but too much in the early stages is worse than too little. The necessary skill, knowledge and manual dexterity must be acquired gradually rather than rapidly, or there will be both frustration and danger.

Most beginners want to produce finished articles, rather than practise the basic techniques. This is natural, but rather like wanting to play tunes before the necessary basic musical knowledge has been acquired. It is advisable to leave the production of specific artefacts until the basic cuts can be performed with a reasonable degree of expertise. There must be a full understanding of the tools, which will begin to feel like extensions of the hands after sufficient practice. The big problem is that if beginners fall into the trap of trying to make *things* before they can execute the basic cuts correctly, their attention will be too much concentrated upon the shape. This is a little like trying a cross-country flight in an aircraft when one is still conscious of flying the thing, and perhaps wondering if the wings are level!

Certain points are emphasised in this book, and some are introduced more than once. This is quite deliberate, these being points which are essential to safety, to an understanding of the fundamentals, or both.

Some newcomers are put off by the fact that woodturning is a craft, and feel that it is perhaps presumptuous of them to try to become craftsmen. My dictionary states that a craftsman is 'one who follows a craft'. If that is so we are all craftsmen, from the very first day, but the point here is that the word requires qualification. We want to be good craftsmen, master craftsmen, or whatever. Some people do fail to achieve skill in this craft, but the root of their problem is usually indolence. As someone once remarked, success is a measure of effort. If there is insufficient effort, there will be inadequate progress. The failures often say that craftsmen are born, not made, but I do not accept this. A reasonably intelligent person, with the will to learn, given good instruction, can pick up enough knowledge in two days to enable shavings to be brought from the wood, leaving a near-perfect finish. This may sound unlikely, but I have proved it more times than I care to remember.

After a short period of instruction, assuming the instructor to have been good at his job, the beginner who devotes sufficient time to regular practice will make rapid progress. The emphasis, however, is on 'regular'. Frequent short periods at the lathe will be far more effective than occasional marathon sessions. Continuity is the key, if possible using the lathe at least once a day, even if only for ten minutes. I am not suggesting that the whole craft can be mastered in a few weeks or months, in fact the more one learns, the more one finds is yet to come, but the basics are by no means as difficult as some would have us believe. Once the fundamentals of the craft are understood, the back of the learner's task has been broken.

For safe and reasonably rapid acquisition of skill, four factors must be considered. These are briefly mentioned here, but are dealt with in detail later in the book.

First, there is the *function* of a tool, or indeed functions. In order to carry out a woodturning operation in an effective and safe manner, it is necessary to use the correct tool.

Second, if that tool is to carry out its appointed function easily and efficiently, it is imperative that it be ground to an acceptable shape.

Third, there is edge sharpness: the achievement and maintenance of an edge which will sever the fibres of the wood cleanly and without bruising.

The fourth point is that the tools must be correctly manipulated by manual skill, and correctly presented to the wood at all times. Only by such accurate presentation and skilled manipulation can satin smooth surfaces which require no abrasive paper be produced.

This book deals with the more simple types of work on the woodturning lathe, as one would expect a guide for beginners to do, but once readers have gained some experience they may like to move on to a more advanced book of mine, *The Manual of Woodturning*, also published by Pelham Books.

Safety-A Warning

Woodturning lathes are among the least dangerous of woodworking machines, in that they have no rotating blades or cutters, as is the case with circular saws, planers and similar workshop equipment. It is necessary to point out, however, that although the lathe does not present the same degree of potential danger, it *can* cause injury to operator or spectators if sufficient care is not exercised. Beginners are therefore strongly advised to follow the instructions given in this book with care, and not to contravene them in any way.

1 The Woodturning Lathe

There is only one way for anyone, male or female, young or old, to become a woodturner in the true sense of the word. That way is by mastering the cutting techniques and resorting to scraping methods only when forced to do so by considerations of safety. This point will be fully explained later, but it must be understood that scraping methods are invariably inferior to the cutting of wood by means of sharp edges, in that a scraped surface will be extremely rough, requiring considerable abrasive work to produce a semblance of smoothness. This is a lengthy and dusty business, and is itself inefficient, since the sanding will almost certainly degrade the fine detail on the job, and in many cases the scraping will be found to have knocked small pieces out of the timber. The objective must be to *cut* the wood cleanly at all times, with tools which are correctly shaped and sharpened, so that maximum smoothness of surface is achieved. Wood turned between centres should require very little abrasive work – in most cases none. Good tools will help, the cheaper and nastier versions should be avoided. There is no necessity to purchase vast numbers of woodturning tools – in fact most people could manage very well with no more than a dozen at most – but it is worth buying the best. Good tools are a delight to use, hold their edges well, and

have that inexplicable quality of feeling 'right' as they cut.

Since this book is intended for those who are new to the craft, and about to set out on the long but fascinating road to skill, we should perhaps have a working definition of woodturning. It is important here that those who have some knowledge of metal-turning should appreciate how far removed it is from the woodturner's art. Metal-turning is a mechanical process, in which a machine is set to perform a certain function. Woodturning, on the other hand, is entirely dependent upon the manual skill of the turner for the shaping of the material. The machine does nothing for the woodturner apart from causing the wood to rotate. Acceptable results in this craft depend upon good tools, properly shaped and sharpened, and upon their correct freehand application and manipulation. It is the need for this high degree of manual skill that makes the craft both difficult and fascinating. My aim in this book is to expose the problems which face beginners, and to give as much assistance as can be given through the medium of the printed word. Naturally there is no real substitute for a period of practical instruction, and indeed books do make a great deal more sense after such an experience. A couple of days with a qualified and experienced instructor can give tremendous help to a beginner in coping with the inevitable problems, and in terms of safety alone it is well worth while. Those who require further details of this should telephone me on 0225 22617.

The range of tools, lathes, and ancillary equipment which faces the newcomer to the craft can cause problems, since it is impossible to be sure of making wise purchases without expert guidance. Just as there are more gadgets made to catch fishermen than to catch fish, there are now too many items being manufactured for woodturners which they would be well advised to avoid. There is perhaps some advantage in being short of cash – and so forced to avoid the purchase of gimmicks which do not promote progress. As in other crafts, such as woodcarving, magnificent work can be done with a few tools and the bare essentials in the way of ancillary equipment. What matters is *skill*, not gadgetry.

My intention in this chapter is to have a look at lathes, and discuss their individual parts; to indicate the range of cutting and scraping tools; and to give some idea of the supporting equipment now available. Where woodturning lathes are concerned one generally gets what one pays for, but it will always be advisable to purchase a machine which is likely to suit the intentions of the turner. If the machine is merely to be a toy, used occasionally for light work and not for serious woodturning, then one of the lower echelon machines may serve. Those who have any serious interest in learning the craft, and particularly those who may be looking to augmenting their incomes or entering into the commercial areas of woodturning, should buy the best that funds will allow. The hobbyist can work with pieces of timber which are comfortably within the lim-

its of the machine, but the man or woman wishing to compete with the commercial turners needs to be able to accept as much as possible of the work which is available, and it soon becomes obvious in such situations that one is usually offered jobs that no one else wants! The point to note here is that a lathe to be used in a commercial situation needs to be able to deal with large and heavy workpieces, long timber and blanks which for one reason or another are out of balance. Heavy lathes are expensive, but they are the ones to choose if your intentions are serious.

If funds are not freely available for those beginning in the craft there is no need to despair, since the acquisition of skill in the essential areas, such as mastery of the basic cutting techniques, is quite possible with a small and inexpensive lathe provided its limitations are not exceeded. The embryo turner needs a machine which will rotate the wood, and a few tools. Given these, a great deal of progress can be made, and once the fundamentals are understood and some satisfactory progress has been made, the machine can be upgraded. Woodturning lathes hold their prices wery well, and secondhand ones are scarce, so the financial loss in such a changeover should not be large.

Lightweight Lathes

The bottom end of the range is represented by the attachments for electric drills, and these should not be despised. The power available is not great, and the little machine is not intended to swing huge baulks of timber, but if used sensibly, within its limitations, it can be an excellent way to explore the foothills of the craft. Those wishing to go higher will soon find themselves moving on to a heavier

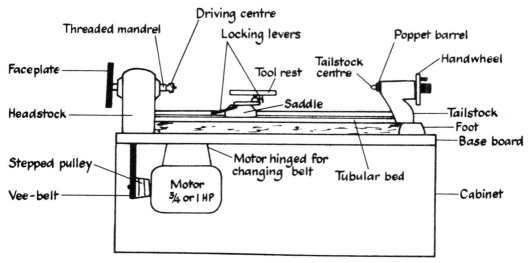

A simple woodturning lathe.

lathe. It should be noted that there are small tools available for use with small lathes, in particular the drill attachments, and these should be used in preference to the larger versions which are employed in general turning. Big tools used on small lathes, which have low power, will over-load the motor and lead to its early failure.

There is another area in which the very light lathes can score over their bigger brothers, which is portability. I am not suggesting that one is likely to want to carry a lathe around, but for those who have no workshop, and for the many flat-dwellers who would like to take up the craft, these light machines provide a very good answer. They can be kept out of sight when not in use, and set up fairly quickly on a suitable table when required. Not the ideal situation, but at least it en-ables people to get started, and to acquire some of the basic skills. These small lathes should be used with the special sets of miniature tools mentioned earlier, but it is not advisable to use these little tools on big machines other than on very small workpieces.

Safety

The two aspects of the craft which will most concern a beginner are safety and efficiency. They are also the two aspects which most concern me, and I am writing in my forty fifth year as a turner, so their importance cannot be over-emphasised. Safety is, of course, of paramount importance, but I have no wish to give the impression that this is a dangerous craft. Certainly there are dangerous people in it, but if common sense is used, and the safety points covered in this book are always given consideration, there is no need for any form of accident. need for any form of accident.

Here I should perhaps mention the expression 'dig-in', which is bandied about so much in writings on the craft. I have discovered, in talking to many of my students, and to people at exhibitions, that the exact nature of a dig-in is a mystery to some, who are never quite sure whether they have experienced one yet, or if a bigger and better version is lurking around the next corner. The fact is that the expression covers incidents ranging from minor skids and runs which merely damage the workpiece, to major cases where a tool dives into the wood and perhaps causes injury to the operator. The ability to define the term is of dubious value, what really matters is the acquisition of the necessary skill and understanding to *avoid* the wretched thing, and this I hope to have provided in some measure by the end of the book.

There is no real substitute for proper instruction on a short intensive course, but care should be taken to ensure that this will be based upon cutting the wood cleanly with sharp edges, leaving the surface under the cut smooth and undisturbed, and producing sharp and clear detail. If this is not established beforehand, it may well be that what is 'taught' is merely the scraping approach, followed by long periods of work with abrasives to rectify in some measure the damage suffered by the wood. This hardly merits the name of woodturning, being no more than a substitute for the skills of the craftsman. The use of a scraper can be explained in a matter of minutes, since if the blade is kept flat, so that its full width is in contact with the toolrest, and the tool is either horizontal or pointing downwards, it is being used correctly. Scrapers cannot be dispensed with entirely, but in view of the inferior surface finishes which they produce their use should be restricted to situations where it is not possible to work with the bevels of the cutting tools rubbing on the wood. This point will be clar-

ified later, but it will help if beginners regard scrapers not as woodturning tools, but as poor substitutes for the gouges and chisels.

Headstock Bearings

One very important point when selecting a lathe is that the bearings in the headstock must be of the best possible quality.

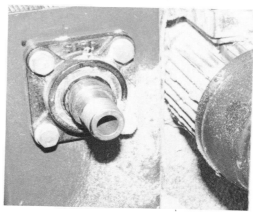

The headstock bearing of the Mini-Max lathe is very solidly built, and easily removed if necessary.

They should permit the rotation of the headstock spindle upon its longitudinal axis, without any other significant movement. There should be no detectable sideways or lateral movement in the spindle, since either of these would adversely affect the work. The drive should also be from the motor to the headstock bearing by means of a belt, together with a series of pulleys which permit speed-changing. Cheap lathes in which the turning is done on the motor shaft itself should be avoided, since the bearings in electric motors are not designed to accept the side and end loadings imposed by the side pressure of the tools and the end pressure from the tailstock. Note also that the use of very small tools on powerful lathes should be avoided by inexperienced workers, since a dig-in can snap a blade and the broken section may fly into the worker's face. When learning this craft, a pair of high-impact goggles, or better still a lightweight visor, should always be worn.

Pulleys

There is another reason for avoiding the type of lathe where the turning is done on the end of the motor shaft, this being that both end- and side-float are normally present to a degree which will affect the turning. The use of belt drives permits rapid and simple speed changing by moving the belt from one pair of pulleys to another. Most woodturning lathes designed for amateur use have pulley blocks on motor shaft and lathe spindle with two,

The speed-change mechanism of the Mini-Max lathe has an automatic belt tension system.

three, or four different sizes of pulleys on each. If the pulley size is the same on the motor shaft as on the headstock spindle, the speed of the lathe will equate with that of the motor, normally 2850 rpm, or in some cases 1450 rpm.

A larger pulley on the motor shaft will give an increase in the rate of rotation, while a small pulley driving a larger one gives a speed less than that of the motor.

Beginners will be well advised to adjust the tension of the driving belt so that it is quite slack, provided this is not taken to the point where the belt will slip on the pulleys under normal load. The correct setting can quite easily be established by a process of trial and error, and a slack belt will protect the novice by greatly reducing the danger of a dig-in. The work will simply cease to rotate, due to slipping of the belt on the drive pulley. In such a situation the tool can be withdrawn from the wood quite safely and the cut started again.

Woodturning lathes are very much alike

An adaptor such as this enables chucks designed for other makes of lathe to be used.

in most respects, differing only in details, and the drawing on page 11 gives a clear idea of the layout of a typical example. Some lathes form the basis for what have come to be known as universal woodworking machines, in that they can be fitted with a range of attachments such as circular saw, planing machine, mortiser, disc sander, belt sander and the like. There are advantages and disadvantages in this, but it is worth noting that the trend over the past few years has been away from the idea of the lathe as a basis for a universal machine.

Lathe Speed

Most modern lathes offer three, four, or sometimes five speeds, taken through stepped pulleys from an electric motor. A half-horsepower motor is powerful enough for normal hobby turning, but a full, or even one-and-a-half, horsepower motor may be needed if the machine is to be used commercially for long periods, often on heavy workpieces.

The switch is the 'no volt overload' type which switches itself off in the event of power failure. The motor and mountings are easily detachable from the rest of the lathe for transport or storage.

The question of speed is a controversial one which I will deal with in more detail later, but it is by no means as important as some people seem to think. What is important is that the headstock should be a heavy-duty item, with bearings of the highest quality for its spindle. These bearings will have to take a great deal of heavy punishment without complaint, and economy is sometimes carried too far by manufacturers who supply bearings which are not suitable for the job and which soon begin to wear and develop undesirable side- and end-float. This is not likely to occur with the middle-to-upper range of machines, but the cheap ones can be a real nuisance.

Tailstock

The tailstock must be of a quality which complements that of the headstock, and it should sit like a rock on the lathe bed once its clamp has been tightened. Any movement at either end of the workpiece will affect the turning. The tailstock can be slid along the lathe bed and locked in any desired position by means of its locking lever. Protruding from the front of the main tailstock casting is the poppet barrel, which can be extended or withdrawn by turning the handwheel, and there is provision for locking it once it has been set. The inside of the poppet barrel, like that of the mandrel, will usually be hollow, and tapered to accept the shanks of drive and tailstock centres, chucks and other equipment. These tapers are described as Morse number 1, 2, or sometimes 3. 'Morse' is an engineering term which, with the number, describes the size and shape of a taper. The larger the number, the heavier the section of the taper.

Tailstocks must be robust. Both the Mini-Max (*left*) and the Tyme Avon (*right*) qualify well.

Lathe Bed

The bed of the lathe will also carry either one or two 'saddles' if the bed itself is circular in section, these saddles providing flat platforms to accept the 'banjos' (toolrest holders). Lathes which do not have round sectioned beds do not normally require saddles, the banjos being placed directly upon the bed. When selecting a lathe, make sure that the banjos are long enough to be usable on large-diameter work, and that the pins of the toolrests are long enough to permit the raising of the toolrest sufficiently for large work between centres.

Toolrest

Most lathes are supplied with one short toolrest, with a single central pin, and a longer one which has two pins may also be available. The latter of course fits into both toolrest holders, and is for use on long work between centres. Toolrests themselves are frequently produced in shapes which appear to have been carefully designed to obstruct the free movement of the tools, and to make life as difficult as possible for the turner. This, of course, is unlikely to be the case, and the undesirable shapes found in the majority of toolrests are probably no more than the result of their being made by engineers for use by woodworkers. The problem can be overcome by having toolrests made up to one's own specification, which is my own approach, but the point of course is that this should not be necessary.

Drive Centres

Two types of driving centre (normally referred to as 'drive centres') are in common use, these being either two-pronged or four-pronged. On good lathes centres will have Morse tapered shanks to fit inside the headstock and tailstock spindles. A two-pronged centre is used on most work, since it is easier to achieve adequate penetration into the end of the wood with this pattern than with the four-pronged

The Lazari Mini-Max T90 lathe, now a very popular model.

The Tyme Avon lathe, man enough to be used regularly by a professional turner.

type, and adequate penetration is important in terms of safety. The two-pronged centre should be used in conjunction with a pointed tailstock centre – a cone shape – these two being a pair for general work. When the material is thin, as in the turning of rails for the backs of chairs for example, there is a danger that a two-pronged centre may cause it to split at some stage during the turning, and for such work a four-pronged type is used,

with a ring or cup centre at the tailstock end. These form a pair for thin work, and greatly reduce the danger of splitting.

The majority of lathes are supplied with a 'dead centre' for the tailstock. This does not revolve with the wood, but remains stationary as the work rotates upon its cone-shaped nose. A great deal of frictional heat is developed, which can lead to enlargement of the hole in the end of the wood and to burning of the workpiece.

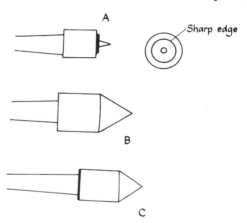

A variety of tailstock centres: A – ring centre; B – revolving centre, which runs on ball bearings; and C – dead centre as supplied with a new lathe. This does not turn with the work.

The problem is overcome by lubricating the tailstock centre from time to time and tightening it a little as required. The lubricant used should not be oil or grease, as sometimes recommended, but a sliver of beeswax or a dab of wax polish. The alternative for those who do not want this problem is the use of a 'live', or rotating, centre, the head of which revolves on ball bearings. Since the head is going round with the wood, there is no friction, and once set up this type of tailstock centre can be ignored until the job is finished.

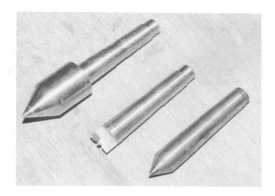

top Revolving tailstock centre. *middle* Two-pronged drive centre. *bottom* Dead centre for tailstock.

Live centres, if of good quality, are expensive, and although they may be desirable they are not essential.

New drive centres, as supplied with the lathe, should be examined and a note made of their shape, so that a file can be used to reshape them when necessary and to keep their edges sharp so that they will penetrate the wood easily. They are made of relatively soft steel, and they have a rough life, so they do become blunt and misshapen in time.

Lighting

Lighting in the workshop is very important and should be considered when the lathe is installed. Strip lighting is fine for general illumination, but it is very diffuse, and there is nothing quite like an ordinary bulb hanging over the machine or a good adjustable lamp.

Eye Protection

If the instructions in this book are followed carefully, there will not be pieces of wood flying around the workshop, but the possibility of something flying from the lathe can never be ruled out completely, so a pair of goggles or a light-weight face visor is a sensible precaution. Ordinary spectacles will deal adequately with small chips, but if these are to be relied upon their lenses should be of safety glass. Goggles should be worn when using the grinder, and when polishing with liquid polishes, drops of which harden quickly and are not easy to remove from spectacle lenses.

Rotating Headstock

Some lathes, like the Tyme models shown in the photographs, provide a means of rotating the complete headstock through up to 90 or even 180 degrees, and this can be a very useful facility. The illustrations show how the lathe can be used with the headstock in various positions which facilitate the turning of large discs, or the hollowing of items such as vases or tankards.

Stability

In the case of a beginner particularly, the stability of the lathe is an important consideration. Vibration must be reduced to a minimum, and the machine should be quiet and sweet in operation. Bolting it firmly down to the floor will help a great deal in these respects, but when this operation is carried out the machine should be set up so that its drive centre is at elbow height for the person who is to use it. This will enable the operator to stand erect without any bending of the back, which would lead rapidly to backache.

2 The Tools

So much for the lathe itself, but there are some very important basic matters to be dealt with before we begin working on the machine. The tools which are to be used in the shaping of the wood are of the greatest importance, and care should be taken in selecting them. Good tools are not expensive, whereas cheap ones will turn out to be so in the long run, and they are often a complete waste of time and money. A lot of valuable time and effort will be expended on them in vainly trying to retain their cutting edges, and the use of poor tools can be most frustrating.

For the complete beginner I normally suggest a set of tools, which I put together as a set for teaching purposes many years ago and which are the tools I use on my courses. The set is made up of nine tools, but only four or five will be really essential in the early stages. Progress will be more rapid for the novice who sets out on spindle-turning, going on to chuck work, and finally to bowls, than for those who try to learn everything at once. For that reason, this book is set out in the order stated, and spindle-turning can be approached with just a few tools. Once

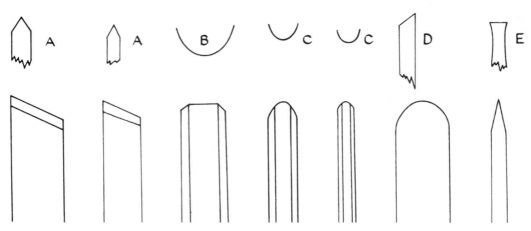

A suitable set of tools for the beginner. Left to right: $1\frac{1}{4}$ in. and $\frac{3}{4}$ in. skew chisels; $\frac{3}{4}$ in. half-round roughing gouge; $\frac{1}{2}$ in. and $\frac{1}{4}$ in. spindle gouges; round – nosed scraper; parting tool. Other tools, such as a square – nosed scraper, may be added as required.

these have been mastered, others can be added to the range, and progress should be satisfactory. Good tools are not expensive when their useful life is considered. A medium-sized gouge is likely to last a hobbyist turner for most of his life, and will give a fair number of years even in the hands of a commercial operator.

It is important to choose good tools, the best available, and there is no need to worry about specially shaped handles until the tools can be used well. Few professionals worry much about handles, though beginners like to make their own fancy shapes, and there is something to be said for long handles which can be steadied against the body when engaged on large workpieces. It is difficult to write a book of this nature without referring fairly frequently to beginners, or novices. This is not in any sense derogatory; we were all beginners once, so I hope that I may be forgiven.

Anyone making a start in this craft should try hard to avoid the common mistake of acquiring too many tools too soon. It is far better to learn the correct use of the few essential ones first, and to practise with them until they feel like extensions to the arms, adding others as and when the need arises.

New tools have a shape of some sort ground on them at the factory, but this shape is unlikely to be what the turner needs, and here we come to one of the most vital issues. Unless and until the technique of grinding the tools is mastered, little progress will be made. A very full and detailed description of the grinding procedure for woodturning tools is vital if this book is to be really helpful, and I will provide it, but I would emphasise that the subject will always be controversial, because so many beginners simply do not understand the underlying truths. It is easy to burn the edges of the tools on the grinder if certain things are not as they should be – and the plaintive letters which so frequently appear in woodworking magazines on the subject of tool grinding bear witness to the fact.

Many newcomers to woodturning bring with them knowledge of the sharpening of tools for other forms of woodwork, which they are reluctant to relinquish, which is unfortunate. There are certain differences in the freehand use of cutting tools in woodturning, as compared to other forms of woodwork, which are vitally important and must be understood unless a great deal of time is to be wasted in producing edges which are unsuitable for lathe work. In view of the supreme importance to the woodturner of being able to produce edges which will shear the shavings away, leaving a satin-smooth surface, I have devoted a section at the end of this chapter to the grinding process. This section is an explanation of the manner in which I sharpen my own tools, and the method has been arrived at over a long period of time during which I have tried many approaches. The controversy over whether or not an oilstone should be used will rage indefinitely, but it is worth noting that the correspondence in magazines which supports this system is largely from people who are still at the learning stage, and who may well change their ideas as time passes. I have no wish to convert anyone to my methods, but I find them satisfactory and they are used without exception by all the well-known demonstrators and writers. I suggest they be tried, and compared with the oilstone method which I have described. The choice then lies with the individual.

Safe and Efficient Cutting

The aim in this craft is to be able to *cut* the wood to shape, leaving the smoothest possible finish on the work. This is not difficult after sufficient practice, but there are three rules which must be followed if safety and maximum efficiency are to be achieved. These rules are listed below. The first two are commonly quoted, and relate to cutting tools only. The third is one which I produced for the benefit of my students many years ago, and it relates to *all* tools used in shaping the wood, including scrapers, old files and what have you.

> **Rule 1:** The bevel must rub the wood.
> **Rule 2:** All cuts must be 'downhill'.
> **Rule 3:** Only that part of any cutting edge which is receiving direct support from the toolrest can safely be used.

Rule 1, then, refers to chisels, gouges, and parting tools (which are chisels). It should be made clear that whilst it is important for the area of the bevel immediately surrounding the part of the edge which is cutting to rub the wood, it is usually essential for the rest of the bevel to be kept clear.

Rule 2 means that all cuts must be made from a larger diameter towards a smaller, assuming that there is a diameter differential. This is usually said to be because if a cut is made 'uphill' it will be against the lie of the fibres, and so will produce a rough surface. In fact the more important point is that it is frequently impossible to *cut* uphill without breaking Rule 3.

In Rule 3 I have selected the words with care, and the sentence means exactly what it says. If any attempt is made to cut with an unsupported part of the edge of a gouge or a chisel, the tool will be dragged into the wood. This can be tried out with the lathe switched off, by placing a tool on the toolrest and rotating the wood by hand, applying different parts of the edge to the wood and observing the results. If an unsupported part engages with the wood, the tendency to dig in will be evident.

Angle of Attack

The illustrations will make it clear that if the handle of a cutting tool is held too low, the angle of attack of the bevel to the work will be insufficient, and there will be no cut. If the handle is held too high, the carefully sharpened edge will be scraping the wood rather than cutting it, and the tool will be blunt in a very short time. The surface produced will be unsatisfactory, and there will be a good chance of a dig-in.

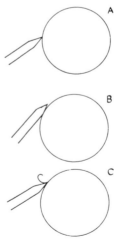

A – Handle held too high – edge scrapes. B – Handle too low, edge does not touch wood. C – Correct – tool removes a shaving.

When the angle of attack is just right, the edge will penetrate the wood by the required amount, removing a shaving, with a part of the bevel rubbing the wood *under the shaving*, and so supporting the cutting edge. This is the only correct situation in terms of application of cutting tools to the wood in woodturning.

Woodturning, when carried out correctly, produces shavings, not dust. Dust is the product of scraping techniques, and of abrasive paper, and is to be avoided as much as possible.

The 'Correct' Speed ...

There are two beliefs commonly held by beginners, and encouraged to some extent by ill-informed writers. These relate to the 'magic angle', and the 'magic speed'. I constantly find when working at exhibitions that people are obsessed with the specific speed at which I am running the lathe (which I frequently do not know) and the angles ground on my tools (which I certainly do not know). Amazement is expressed when I say that I am not particularly interested in the speed of the lathe in terms of precise rpm, nor in the exact angle ground on any specific tool, but both statements are quite true, and I will explain the reasons fully.

The question of speed seems to be a great problem to many people, but in fact the answer is that the lathe should be run at a speed which seems appropriate – in other words, a speed which suits the turner. If the work is rotated too fast, the cut will be dusty, and the edges of the tools will rapidly be overheated. If the turner uses a speed which seems right, this allows for his degree of confidence, and competence. It may be that after a few months of practice he will find himself moving up

the speed range a little. The thing to remember is that there is no correct speed, and never can be, for work which varies in diameter. Experienced turners can work fast, moving the tools along the wood at a surprising rate, therefore they can afford to run the lathe faster than those whose tool movement is slow, since 'rate of feed' with the tool needs to be related to the speed of rotation.

... and the 'Right' Angle?

Regarding the bevel angles of the cutting tools, and indeed of the scrapers, a little thought will show that there can never be a fixed angle which is right for every turner. If the tools are ground to produce a wide bevel there will be a very fine edge which may be suitable for soft wood but which will soon be destroyed by hard timbers; and frictional heat against the wood will soon cause burning of the metal, since the very thin edge cannot dissipate the heat fast enough. If the bevels are ground very steeply, so that they are not wide, there will be plenty of strength and heat dissipation at the cutting edge, but very little sharpness. Any angle chosen for the bevel is therefore a compromise between sharpness and strength. In addition to this, a long bevel will require the tool handle to be held very low, if the bevel is to

A – With a long bevel the handle must be held low. B – Shorter angle of bevel, handle must be raised.

rub the wood while the tool is cutting, whereas a short bevel will dictate that the handle be held higher.

It is also important to realise that there must be only *one* bevel on a woodturning tool; there is no second bevel at the edge as with a woodworking chisel. Reference to the illustrations will show that the bevel either runs dead straight, if it has been ground on the side of the wheel, or is hollow-ground, if it has been ground on the curved face. The former is acceptable, the latter preferable, but a convex bevel is almost never right and will give trouble in most situations. There is one exception to this; some people do grind convex bevels on gouges which they keep for use on the insides of bowls so that the convex bevel gives good support to the cutting edge as it works on the concave surface.

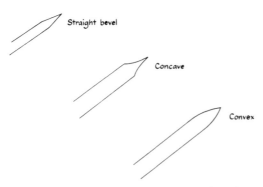

Top: A straight bevel will do, as produced on side of wheel. *Centre:* Hollow ground bevel is best, as from grinding on front face of stone. *Bottom:* Avoid any suggestion of a convex outline like this.

The reason for having no second bevel on woodturning tools is really quite simple. We have already noted that the bevels rub the work beneath the shaving, so sup-porting the cutting edges and preventing the dreaded dig-in. If a second bevel is formed, it will be found necessary to lift the tool handle and support the cutting edge by means of the smaller bevel adjacent to the cutting edge, which is usually an inadequate support area.

SHARPENING WOODTURNING TOOLS

I did say that the subject of sharpening woodturning tools is a controversial one, and this is indeed the case, but here I will do two things. First, I will describe in detail the methods I use, and second, I will describe methods which can be used by those who choose to do so. It is not an easy matter to change the fixed opinions of those who have been raised on the idea that an oilstone produces a 'better edge', and I have no desire to do so. The real question is, of course, what is a 'better' edge? What is produced when woodturning tools are honed is a *finer* edge, and this is not what we need. A very fine edge is sought by all carvers, and I would never dream of trying to use a carving tool straight from a grinder, but there is a difference which must be appreciated. This is that the work done by turning tools is quite unlike that performed by tools which are hand held in other forms of woodwork, because there is a high degree of frictional heat produced as the bevels rub on the rapidly rotating timber, and the relative speed between the wood and the edge is many times higher than in other woodworking operations. In a very few minutes a woodturning tool operating on a 3- or 4-inch diameter cylinder rotating at 2,000 rpm or so can bring off many yards of shavings. The edges must therefore be right for the purpose. When an 80-grit wheel is used, the edges will have a very fine 'bite', or invisible saw-toothed quality, which is ideal for the purpose.

Grinding Tools

In order to be able to produce these edges, and to use the tools straight off the stone, it is necessary to understand the grinding process. It is evident from the correspondence in magazines on this subject that many people do not understand the process properly, and so complain of burned edges. The thousands of people who have watched me turning will be aware that I keep the tools on the wheel until they are fully ground, and do not use any water for cooling purposes. This is the case at every exhibition, and in my workshop, so there can be little doubt on the point.

Use of a 'devil stone', or dressing stick, to keep the wheel flat and in good cutting condition.

A grindstone which is to be used for the shaping and sharpening of woodturning tools must be flat across its face, and must

be regularly dressed with a carborundum dressing stick, or 'devil stone', to keep it sharp and free from impacted resin and dust. The tools should *not* be placed on the toolrest of the grinder, because if this is done there will be difficulty in judging the very light pressure which must exist between bevel and stone. Finally, there must be no attempt to place the bevels correctly on the grinding wheel – the heel of the bevel is applied lightly to the wheel, the handle held low, then the handle is raised as the edge is brought down the wheel. This procedure stops when the edge is *almost* touching the surface of the stone, but not quite. If the tool is a gouge, a rolling action is performed until sparks have been seen all along the edge, and the job is done. In the case of a chisel there is obviously no rolling action, but the tool may need to be moved slowly from side to side, to make sure that all the edge is ground.

If the grindstone is kept in first-class condition, and only the weight of the tool is applied to it, without pressure, the tool will not be overheated. Those who find themselves unable to cope with this system may, however, be forced to use oil-stones, so I am including some comments on procedure. Before going on to this, I would like to point out one common error which may be found in writings about woodturning, which is the suggestion that it may be beneficial to grind the tools almost, but not quite, to the edge, finishing the job off on an oilstone. A little thought will show that if this system is adopted, a problem will arise. If the grinding is stopped short of the cutting edge, there will obviously be a small unground strip between the ground bevel and the cutting edge. Since the surface of the bevel is hollow ground, the oilstone touches only the

Grinding a small gouge. Note that the tool does not contact the grinding rest. A smooth rolling motion is employed, with light pressure.

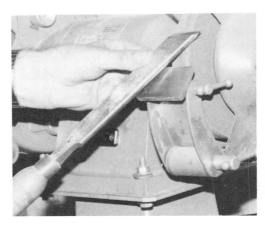

The edge of a skew chisel is kept square across the wheel. Do not put the blade on the grinding rest.

Grinding a spindle gouge. Keep the blade just clear of the grinding rest. The profile of the spindle gouge is a slow curve.

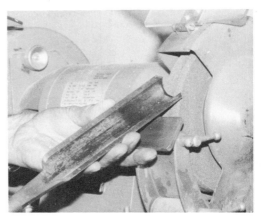

A roughing gouge is rolled from side to side. There is no contact with the grinding rest, and the edge is maintained square to the sides of the blade.

cutting edge and the heel of the bevel, and at both points a small 'flat' will be formed. The flat area formed at the cutting edge is now the bevel, and the tool must be op-

erated on this totally inadequate area if it is to cut.

If water is used to cool tools during the grinding process – which should not be necessary – care must be taken to ensure that *warm* tools only are treated in this way. The immersion of *hot* tools in cold water is an extremely bad practice, which ruins the temper of the steel and destroys its qualities of edge retention. It is better to learn how to use the grinder, since once this procedure becomes instinctive, there will be no need for coolant.

As the grinding and general sharpening of tools is a matter of extreme importance to any beginner, we have to decide how the various types of tool should be dealt with. There is also the very pertinent question asked by many students, regarding the moment when tools need sharpening. The best guide here is to say that if the worker is wondering whether or not a tool requires sharpening, it probably does. If he or she is not wondering about the matter, the tool is likely to be performing satisfactorily. In other words, 'if in doubt, sharpen'. The process takes a very short time indeed once one has become adept at it, and woodturning tools do require frequent sharpening, simply because they do a colossal amount of work in a relatively short time, and are subjected to a high-speed battering by the timber plus a lot of frictional heat if the bevels are rubbing the wood as they should be.

If the sharpening process is carried out correctly, very little metal is removed in restoring an edge, and although the turner appears to be sharpening tools extremely frequently, they do last a very long time. Only a skim is taken from a tool in sharpening, no more than would be removed if the operation were carried out with an oilstone.

Gouges are held with the bevel on the stone at the required angle, which is established by putting the heel on first, with the handle low, then bringing the tool

down the wheel and raising the handle until the edge is almost touching the wheel surface. The tool is then rolled slowly from side to side without pressure, until sparks have been seen at all points along the cutting edge. There is no need to swing the handle from side to side in an arc, as some beginners do; this serves merely to make the procedure appear more difficult than it really is, and to provide some form of exercise for the turner.

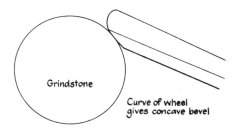

Correct position for grinding a gouge on face of wheel, roll tool slowly from side to side.

Parting tools are treated as narrow chisels, but they are manufactured with edges which are wider than the thickness of the blade. This provides relief behind the cutting edge, so that the tool does not bind in the cut and become overheated. This shape will disappear in time, with repeated sharpening, but binding in the cut can be avoided by widening the cut itself with the corner of the tool. In other words, one cuts until the tool is felt to be binding, then the tool is withdrawn and the cut is widened by means of a fine cut with a corner, so that the original cut can be continued. These tools are used for a variety of purposes, but they produce poor surface finishes. This is not important if the surface will not show in the completed turning, or if other tools are to be used after the parting tool.

Scrapers are a completely different matter, and in view of the poor finishes they produce I would dearly love to be able to say that they should not be used at all. This, however, would be wrong, since the real function of a scraper is to take over when other tools have become unsafe in use, which will normally be because the shape of the workpiece precludes any possibility of keeping the bevel of the cutting tool in contact with the wood. If one considers the shape of a brandy glass, or a bowl which curls inward at the top, it will be noted that such shapes cannot be completed with a gouge because the back of the tool will eventually strike the rim of the bowl, preventing bevel contact, and if the gouge is used beyond this point there is likely to be a severe dig-in.

I am often asked why it is that cabinet-makers use scrapers to achieve the final finish, whereas woodturners find their scrapers very poor substitutes for cutting tools. The fact is that whilst the woodturner's scraper 'cuts' in a similar manner to that of the cabinet-maker, the woodturner is not able to restrict the action of his scraper to movement along the grain of the wood. The cabinet-maker bends his scraper slightly and pushes it slowly along the wood, working with the grain. The turner, whose work is rotating, tears the surface of the timber as the tool works across the grain. Woodturning scrapers are inefficient by comparison with gouges and chisels, but if properly sharpened they are at their best when working into end grain, where they should be taking off definite shavings.

A scraper can take over when a cutting tool can no longer be used safely simply because the bevel of a scraper never touches the wood – indeed if it did so the tool could not cut. Little skill is required in the use of these tools, which unfortunately leads to their being used far too frequently by unskilled workers, often producing surfaces which are not really satisfactory even after considerable abrasive treatment. It is therefore not a good idea to have too many scrapers during the learning period: the temptation to use them when a cutting tool should really be employed is likely to be too great. I would suggest one square-ended scraper for levelling recesses, such as in the centres of plates or trays, and one round-nosed scraper for general hollowing. The bevel angle of a scraper is not critical but, as with cutting tools, a long bevel will produce a fine edge which can be very sharp but which will not last long, while a narrow bevel will give great strength but with reduced cutting efficiency.

Scrapers are always used with negative rake, that is the handle is always held a little higher than the tip of the blade, and the tool is kept flat on the toolrest. There is little skill involved, it being necessary only to know that the tool is inclined downwards, kept flat on the toolrest and never pushed hard at the wood. If a scraper is pointed upwards, particularly inside a bowl, there is a very real danger of a nasty accident, which may break the tool and fling the broken section out at the turner. The scraper is a 'last resort' tool for those who are capable of using gouges and chisels efficiently.

It is possible, though in my view undesirable, to make scrapers from old files, an idea which originated in an old book on the craft. Scrapers are the least expensive of the turner's tools, and they are toughened and tempered by experts. Files are brittle, and unless 'normalised' by heating and cooling they are quite capable of snapping if subjected to sudden strain. The thought of a broken piece of a file being flung out of a rotating bowl is not one I care to dwell upon. There is some case for the making-up of the odd 'form tool' from a file, if the result is to be used in a situation where there is little projection over the edge of the toolrest. I am thinking here of tools made up for the final trimming of certain details in repetition work, such as the production of chess pawns, or a particular detail perhaps on the foot of an egg cup. This sort of thing does not, however, work quite as well as may be expected, and can sometimes damage fine detail rather than improve it. Form tools are not used to produce the shape, merely to trim it lightly once it has been turned.

The Oilstone

It is a sad fact that those beginners who do not obtain any proper instruction in the use of a grinder for shaping and sharpening woodturning tools will have problems, and in many cases they will revert to using oilstones. Some regard an oilstone as a far more craftsmanlike tool than a grinder, and find it appealing because it does not produce showers of sparks, or burn the edges of their tools. I went through all this, and did stone my tools for quite a long period back in the 'forties and early 'fifties. I would do it now if I could find any advantage, which I cannot, but I will describe the procedure for the benefit of those who elect to employ it.

Oilstones will not replace the grinder, which must be mastered even by those who adopt the honing system, because tools have to be ground to shape when new, and reground when they have lost their correct shape as a result of consider-able use. Those who do wish to use oilstones between grindings will need two oilstone slips, not one, because one must be kept for the gouges, which will wear hollows in its surfaces, and the other restricted to the honing of chisels. There will be no need for the expensive oilstones and slips used by woodcarvers, in fact I would certainly not let my Washita and Arkansas stones anywhere near my turning tools. The cheaper varieties of manufactured stone will serve, and the thing to do is to experiment with various grades, starting with a medium. New oilstone slips need a good soaking in a mixture of paraffin and thin oil, about half-and-half, and this is a good mixture for lubrication of the stone when in use.

The method usually employed in honing woodturning tools with an oilstone slip is simple enough, and there is really only one way to describe the action. In the case of a chisel, the tool is steadied against some convenient object, such as the handwheel of the tailstock, and the oilstone is applied to the heel of the bevel. A circular motion of the stone then begins, and at the same time the stone is slowly tilted forward until oil is seen to creep over the edge of the tool. The temptation to tilt a fraction further, just to be sure, should be avoided. It will be fatal to the object of the exercise, and will ruin the edge.

The honing of a gouge is basically similar, but rather more complicated, since the tool has to be rolled slowly from side to side while the circular motion is performed. Oilstones are not usually used on scrapers, but a coarse one will produce some sort of cutting burr if there is no grinder handy. Do not remove the roughness from the upper surface of the scraper, since it is this which does the 'cutting'.

The grinding of turning tools becomes a simple matter with sufficient practice, but many beginners are quite naturally inhibited by the fear of spoiling tools which they have recently purchased at considerable expense. It is, fortunately, not necessary to practise the grinding on the tools themselves, since scrap metal can be used to very good effect. A visit to a small local engineering firm should produce a few pieces of flat strip steel which can represent chisels, and some rod or tubing which can be used for gouge-grinding practice. The answer lies in using little or no pressure, not putting the tools on the 'grinding rest', and always making sure that the stone is sharp and clean. If in doubt about this, turn the grinding wheel slowly by hand and examine it for any sign of glazing. If such is discovered, use the dressing stick, or 'devil stone'. The use of this requires no skill: it is simply placed on the toolrest of the grinder, pressed firmly against the rotating wheel, and moved gently from side to side. Twenty seconds or so should suffice unless the wheel has been allowed to get into bad condition. New wheels have a sort of skin which is produced in the manufacturing process, and this should be removed by means of the devil stone before the grinder is used on the tools.

3 Tool Functions and Peculiarities

One of the great problems encountered by those who take up the craft of woodturning without proper instruction is that of being unsure whether the tool being used is the correct one for the cut being performed. This is not too easy to overcome, and reading books will not always help since there are now many to choose from and they tend to disagree with one another. This has become so confusing that I now advise my students to restrict their reading on the craft to books and articles written by people who are known to demonstrate in public. The reason for this is that such writers have to be able to show that what they say is correct if called upon to do so, which they frequently are.

Gouges

Roughing gouges, which are square-ended, are used in bringing lengths of wood down from irregular shape to cylindrical form. This includes producing cylinders from squares, octagonal shapes or rough branchwood. Any part of the cutting edge can be used, provided of course that it is receiving direct support from the toolrest, but the corners must be kept clear of the wood. Bringing irregular shapes down to true cylindrical form is known as 'roughing down'. The rapid removal of waste from obvious places to

Start of the roughing-down process on a small square.

Reducing the diameter of a cylindrical blank with a roughing gouge. The angle of the tool to the work must not change during the cut.

29

make a rough approximation of the finished job, is known as 'roughing out'. Beginners should be cautious about the use of these tools in hollows, an operation which calls for some degree of skill.

Spindle gouges are easily distinguishable from roughing gouges, since they are very shallow in the flute, and are ground with a curved profile, unlike the roughing gouge which is very deep in the flute and ground square. The function of a spindle gouge is the production of convex and concave curves, an operation which the tool will perform extremely well in skilled hands. Projects which are supported at each end, between the lathe centres, are known as 'spindle turnings' or simply as 'spindles', and this type of gouge is used mainly in work of this nature. It is also used in some forms of work where the job is supported at one end only, on a chuck, provided that the grain of the wood is running in the same direction as the lathe bed. The use of these tools on discs, where the grain is running across the lathe bed, is inadvisable until a fair degree of skill has been acquired.

Small spindle gouges, about $\frac{1}{4}$-inch, are used in the initial stages of hollowing end grain, to remove wood rapidly. Such jobs will normally have to be finished off with a round-nosed scraper once it becomes difficult to keep the bevel of the gouge in contact with the wood. These small gouges can also be useful in small hollows, such as on the stems of goblets or egg cups.

Parting Tools

Parting tools have a variety of uses, and since they are very easy to use they are employed far too much by many beginners. This is a pity, because the finish produced by these tools is normally poor, and frequently atrocious. They are used in 'parting off', as in the case of a completed chessman or knob for a cupboard, cutting right through the wood so that the workpiece falls into the waiting hand of the turner. Other uses are recessing circular discs to accept tiles when making cheese boards, cutting round pins, on tool handles or for use as tenons in constructing furniture, and the tool is very useful in the setting out of furniture legs by cutting in at appropriate points to define diameters, so that the turner can concentrate on the shape.

Skew Chisels

Skew chisels are used for smoothing, and for the cutting of details such as beads, V-cuts, fine decorative lines, and the trimming of end grain. The chisel is not more difficult to use than a gouge, but it is certainly a much more difficult tool to master without assistance, being capable of 'digs' which can be both spectacular and alarming.

Scrapers

Round-nosed scrapers are used mainly on end grain, where the job is supported on a faceplate or chuck and requires hollowing. There are many items of this nature, such as goblets, vases, tankards, and boxes of various types. The use of scrapers on spindle projects should be avoided at all costs in view of the dreadful surfaces they create.

Keen woodturners will not allow themselves to be drawn into the trap of using scrapers where cutting tools ought properly to be employed. There are occasions on which their use is correct, in end-grain work, or where the internal shape of a bowl is such that it cannot be followed through safely with a gouge. I am not suggesting that there is no need for scrapers in the craft, merely that their use should be restricted to situations where other tools cannot safely be used.

The occasions on which it will be found necessary to use scrapers between centres will be rare indeed. The action of the tool on spindle work is quite wrong, the fibres of the wood being dragged up and a messy rough surface being left which can only be brought to a smoothish sort of finish by means of lengthy abrasive work. Coarse abrasive paper is needed in these situations, and this will scribe countless deep scratches round the work, which are very difficult to remove.

It is a pity that the process of making scrapers from old files was ever introduced, since there is little requirement for skill in either the making or the using of these things, and they tend to obstruct rather than assist those who are trying to learn the craft. The practice is quite common however, so I will give a brief outline of it. The old file to be used should be fairly thick, and the first step is to grind away the upper surface of the file for an inch or two at the end, to get at the softer metal. When this has been done the profile can be shaped according to requirements. There is nothing critical about the bevel angle, but it should not be so shallow that the file is brought to a thin edge which is not able to carry away the heat, nor so steep as to be incapable of carrying a decent cutting edge.

A special scraping tool which can be useful at times is made from an old file which has been ground to a definite hook at its tip. The use of this tool is quite simple: it is employed in separating a ring

from a piece of turning. When the ring has been released from the main body of the work, it is secured with adhesive tape until the turning and polishing of the remainder is completed, then it is sanded and polished by hand. This is a novelty which beginners soon tire of, its main use as far as I can see being in the production of rattle-type toys for infants.

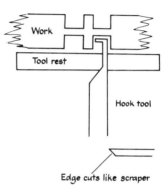

Home-made hook tool for separating rings on spindle work. Made from an old file or scraper, it can be a useful piece of equipment.

Scrapers, if properly sharpened and used in the right situations, do a reasonable job, and we have to accept the fact that true cutting tools cannot be used all the time. The use of scraping techniques with gouges and chisels must be avoided at all costs. This destroys their edges, is likely to lead to severe digs, and produces rough hairy surfaces. Unfortunately there are many people using cutting tools with a scraping action, and most of these are unaware of the fact. Keen cutting edges, suitable for woodturning, must be maintained on the cutting tools at all times, but unless they are allowed to cut, and so produce shavings, they will be scraping and will be blunted very rapidly.

INNOVATIONS IN WOODTURNING EQUIPMENT

This is perhaps as good a point as any to bring in some explanation of the various oddities in the world of woodturning tools. The popularity of this craft has been increasing steadily over the past fifteen years or so, and the result is a very competitive market for the tool manufacturers, who have to try to keep ahead of one another in order to stay in business. In many ways this is good for the craft, but there are two sides to every coin, and some of the items now offered for sale in the woodturning tool and equipment field are of dubious value. Some of this equipment is also very expensive, and I feel that the best advice I can give to beginners is that they should not buy anything until they have established clearly in their minds why they want to buy it.

One problem faced by makers of woodturning tools is that there are remarkably few actual patterns. Unlike the craft of woodcarving, where there are some three thousand known patterns in existence, woodturning has only a dozen or so basic tools and is now in the process of acquiring a few more of doubtful value. Naturally, for each pattern there is a range of sizes, but most turners will need only one, or perhaps two, from each style. It is possible to waste a good deal of money by buying strange objects which appear on the market only to vanish again in a year or so.

I now receive a lot of queries regarding the usefulness or otherwise of tools made from high-speed steel which seems to be receiving rather more attention than it deserves in the woodturning press. This material is very hard by comparison with the normal carbon steel tools, and so takes much longer to sharpen. It is also more difficult for a beginner to cope with on a grinder. High-speed steel tools are much more expensive than their carbon steel counterparts, and in my opinion they do not cut quite as well. The sales line is that they hold their edges longer, and perhaps they do, but since under normal circumstances the sharpening of a carbon steel gouge or chisel takes me around twenty seconds, I am not over impressed by this.

Another area of controversy and misunderstanding exists in connection with tools which are marketed as 'long and strong' or, in the case of some gouges, 'deep, long and strong'. The fact that these tools are longer, stronger, and possibly deeper than others does not necessarily mean that they are better. They are certainly far more expensive, but they are designed for situations in which the projection over the edge of the toolrest is excessive, and could lead to flexing of the blade if a standard tool was used. Such situations are now uncommon in most workshops. 'Long and strong' tools are clumsy in use, and have no sensitivity. There is no 'feel' to them, and, contrary to common belief, they are not popular with professional turners. They have existed together with standard tools for many years, and had they been better it seems reasonable to assume that the former would have vanished from the market.

There is some sense in buying a 'long and strong' gouge for bowl-turning since this is one situation in which there can be considerable projection of the tool over the edge of the toolrest. Many turners do use this type of gouge for bowls, the gouge in question being known as 'deep, long and strong', usually a $\frac{3}{8}$-inch wide version.

This is not essential, however, since there are curved toolrests which can be used as the bowl becomes deeper, so reducing the overhang of the gouge. This is reasonably effective, but there can be an undesirable element of 'bounce' when working near the centre of the bowl, due to the toolrest being supported only at the other end. One gradually becomes accustomed to the fact that answers to problems frequently produce problems of their own.

CUTTING TECHNIQUE

Another annoyance in my life is the much-vaunted long shaving. This was mentioned in an old book on turning, and I am often asked how such phenomena can be produced. The answer, of course, is that they come from wood which has a high moisture-content. A cutting tool which has been correctly sharpened, and which is presented accurately to the work, will always produce a shaving. The length of the shaving will be dependent upon the dampness or otherwise of the wood. If the wood is dry, the shaving will break into short lengths. There is not, as far as I know, a market for long shavings, and their production is not indicative of skill, but those who want some need only turn wet wood.

It is important to realise that the toolrest, and the bevel on the cutting tool, are the only two real friends the woodturner has. Neither, therefore, must be neglected, or there will be a penalty to be paid. Tools, including scrapers and old files, must be in firm contact with the toolrest at all times when cutting. Lifting a tool clear of the toolrest during a cut has been the cause of many an accident. In this connection it is important to observe that it is not essential for the turner's hand to rub against the toolrest, though some writers do advocate the procedure. The tools *must* be on the rest, but contact between rest and hand is optional.

The bevel on a cutting tool has two functions to perform if the tool is being used as it should be. First the bevel, or rather the part of it which surrounds the section of the edge which is cutting, rubs the wood under the shaving, so preventing overcutting or digging-in. Second, and this is not always realised, the bevel forms a pivot point for the tool, permitting the depth of cut to be dictated to the gouge or chisel by increasing or decreasing the angle of attack between bevel and wood.

It is unfortunate that many people fall into the trap of controlling the depth of cut by adding or subtracting pressure. If a tool is cutting too deeply, the pressure is relaxed and the tool is dragged along the wood on its edge. This is quite wrong, leading to violent sideways skids and ridge-infested surfaces. Pressure should be maintained all the time with cutting tools, the depth being a direct function of the angle of attack.

Note also that when a tool has been correctly ground there will be one bevel, and one only, not a series of facets caused by removing the tool from the grinder to cool it or to inspect progress and replacing it at a different angle. Tools should be left in contact with the wheel until the grinding is completed, with little or no pressure, and if the wheel is in good condition there will be no problems.

I am aware of the initial difficulties involved in learning to do this well, but I cannot emphasise enough the fact that once the knack of grinding has been acquired, forty per cent of the student's troubles are over. Unfortunately there is a strong temptation for those who cannot grind tools easily to go on using them long after they have become blunt. The effect of this is disastrous, for that elusive 'professional finish' cannot be obtained by means of blunt tools.

To sum up I would say, keep at it until you find the process easy, and that time will come sooner than you may think. The best advice I can give is that a period should be set aside for grinding practice every time the workshop is visited.

4 Basic Spindle-turning

The reader who has stayed with me so far is probably beginning to wonder when we are going to get down to some woodturning, and will be pleased to know that the time has come.

There are two schools of thought on the teaching of this craft, one being that bowl-turning should be taken first, and the other that one should start with spindle-turning, which is easier on the nerves. This is a matter of preference, and I subscribe to the latter view, so let's have a look at the principles of turning between centres.

Some books and articles advocate the removal of the corners of square lengths of wood which are intended for spindle work, the blank thus being converted to octagonal form. This is perhaps a good idea when young folk are being instructed, but it is not necessary for adult students who can easily learn to remove the corners in the lathe by means of a roughing gouge. If the blank is too large to rotate in the lathe without the corners being removed, as may be the case at times with certain machines, the best tool for the job is a bandsaw, with its table tilted to 45 degrees and the wood run against a fence. I will return to the subject of bandsaws at a later stage, because they are extremely useful in a turner's workshop.

Mounting the Workpiece

No matter what the project may be, *one of the most important aspects of woodturning is the safe and secure mounting of workpieces*, every care being taken to see that there is no chance of their flying from the lathe. Wood which has been correctly prepared and mounted, whether on a faceplate or chuck, or between centres, will not present this sort of danger, and the whole thing is really just a question of common sense. Square lengths of wood which are to be mounted between centres

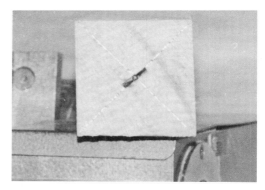

Diagonals are marked on the end of a square blank to find the centre. An old driving centre has been used to prepare the blank for mounting.

35

normally have the diagonals drawn in on their ends to locate the centres, and the end of the blank which is to go on to the drive centre requires special treatment. One of the most important safety aspects in this sort of work is adequate penetration of the drive centre into the wood, and there is no excuse for sloppy work which could cause serious injury to the operator or to an onlooker. Some people, and I am sorry to say that I am one, have a regrettable habit of forcing workpieces on to the drive centre by means of the tailstock. If the wood is really soft, this is acceptable, but the practice is not suitable for hard timbers. Considerable force will be required to mount these, and the strain on the headstock bearing will do the machine no good at all.

The best approach is to have an old drive centre, or a cold chisel of similar width, and to hammer this into the wood on the centre mark to a depth of about $\frac{1}{4}$–$\frac{3}{8}$ inch. The device can then be removed from the wood, which is offered up to the centre in the lathe, and the tailstock is tightened firmly but not excessively so. Another point here is that if a 'live' centre is in use in the tailstock it will soon be damaged if it has to push work on to the drive centre, and rotating tailstock centres are expensive. (The makers of the Avon lathes do in fact offer a suitable tool as an optional extra.)

It is perhaps worth mentioning that under no circumstances should the drive centre itself be hammered into the wood. These items are made from relatively soft steel, and will be damaged by such treatment. It is sometimes suggested that saw cuts should be made across the end of the workpiece to facilitate entry of the drive centre, but this idea is not too clever, since the project often calls for the full length of the wood, and there will be small square holes left at the base by the saw cuts.

When the blank has been mounted in the machine, all the clamps must be checked for tightness, and they should be checked again as a matter of habit before the lathe is switched on. The toolrest is fitted into the banjo, and positioned along the wood a little below centre and reasonably close to the job, and its clamping lever must be tightened firmly. Another point which is sometimes missed is that the lathe should not be run with excessive tailstock pressure, which is bad for the headstock bearing, and may cause whipping of the workpiece as its diameter decreases. Once the tailstock wheel has been tightened fully it can be backed off a quarter of a turn or so.

Toolrest Height

There seems to be considerable confusion among beginners regarding the height at which the toolrest should be set, and a few remarks on this may help at this stage. Like many other issues in this craft, the matter is basically one of common sense, and a little experimenting with a piece of wood in the lathe and the motor switched off will be found very instructive. The points to note are that it is essential for the tool to be in contact with the toolrest, and for the bevel to be rubbing the wood. Since firm contact must be maintained at these two points, it is readily apparent that a high toolrest position means holding the handle of the tool high and cutting well up on the wood, whereas a low toolrest position means a low handle and a low cutting-point. Between centres, the toolrest may be positioned to suit the turner, provided the bevel is kept rubbing and the tool is firmly on the rest.

If a circular disc of wood is mounted in the lathe, on a woodscrew chuck or a faceplate, and a similar experiment is conducted, it will be found that there is an important difference. When cutting across the face of a disc, the cut must run exactly to the centre of the job, with the bevel rubbing and the tool on the toolrest throughout. If this is tried, with the motor switched off, it will clearly be seen that if the toolrest is either too high or too low, the cut cannot run to the centre. There is a danger in this which needs to be pointed out. If the toolrest is too high, as may well be the case with an inexperienced worker, it will become obvious towards the end of the cutting operation that a small disc of wood at the centre will remain uncut. The danger is that the worker may bring up the handle of the gouge to deal with this small area, so lifting the bevel from the wood and causing a dig-in. If the toolrest is too low there will still be an uncut area, since the cut will run to a point below the centre, and here the temptation is to lift the tool from the toolrest to catch that last little piece, again provoking a dig-in. This may sound complicated, but the point will be obvious when tried out on the lathe.

My experience of instructing beginners, which is extensive, indicates clearly that the best approach is one which breaks down the cutting of wood in a lathe so that the fundamental cutting techniques are revealed. When these are clearly explained, and thoroughly understood, only sufficient practice is needed to provide skill in cutting. There is no substitute for this practice, any more than there would be in learning to play a musical instrument, but rapid and satisfactory progress is dependent upon a thorough understanding of the tools and of the ways in which they must be manipulated in the interests of safety and efficiency.

ROUGHING, SMOOTHING AND PLANING

The roughing gouge, which is deep-fluted and square in its profile, is the tool used in these operations. If it has been freshly ground, and is used exactly as described here, there should be few problems, and after a little practice the roughing gouge is likely to become a favourite tool with many workers. Numerous people, however, do not like the look of the roughing down process, and I find this quite understandable. After all, a square length of wood, spinning rapidly in a lathe, does not appear to be the best thing to poke a steel tool into. One should remember that the tool has been evolved for the express purpose of bringing irregular lengths of wood down to a regular cylinder, prior to commencing the shaping of a woodturning project, and in fact once a few points are made clear there is little danger. Many students who come to my workshop are apprehensive when facing this task for the first time, but they are always surprised at the docility of the gouge, and roughing down quickly becomes one of their favourite operations.

The difference between roughing down and roughing out is frequently misunderstood, and requires clarification. Roughing down is the reduction of an irregular *length* of wood to a regular cylinder. It is followed by roughing out, which is the rapid removal of waste from the obvious areas, producing a very rough approximation of the desired shape. Roughing down embraces both the removal of the corners of a square piece of timber and the straightening of other irregular lengths such as pieces of branchwood. When the latter are to be turned, caution should be exercised, and beginners are advised to reduce the speed of the lathe until the worst of the job is done, as there is likely to be vibration. The bark should also be checked, and any loose sections removed before the lathe is started. Some protection for the face is also worth considering, and the best equipment for work of this nature is a lightweight visor.

The most common requirement, however, is the removal of the corners of square turning blanks, prior to commencing the shaping, an operation which is perfectly safe if approached as described here. While bevel angles are not critical, and can be selected to suit the softness or hardness of the wood, a good general-purpose angle for a roughing gouge during the learning period will be about 45 degrees. The corners of squares cannot be seen when the wood is rotating, and it is important to ensure that the tool is placed firmly upon the toolrest before its edge meets the work.

One point which may not be clear when approaching lathe work for the first time is that because of the essential need to support the section of a cutting edge by means of the area of the bevel which lies behind it, there can be difficulty for inexperienced workers when attempting to start a cut at the extreme end of a piece of wood. A little thought will show that in such situations the cutting edge will meet the wood before the bevel, and the tool must travel a short distance before bevel support is available. This means that unless the approach angle of the tool is exactly right there may be a dig-in. After some practice this ceases to be a real problem, but in the reduction of squares to

cylinders there is a danger that if the cut is started at the end of the workpiece and the approach angle is wrong, there may be a dig-in, which can split pieces off the full length of the work, and these pieces may fly up into the turner's face. Again, a visor is a good idea, but the difficulty can be reduced by taking the job in sections, with all cuts running *off* the ends of the wood rather than on to them.

When turning square workpieces extra care should be taken, since a square is potentially more dangerous than a cylinder. Once the wood has been mounted in the machine and all the clamps have been checked for tightness, the workpiece should be rotated by hand to ensure that the corners will clear the toolrest, and the clamp which holds the toolrest in its banjo should be tightened really firmly. The banjo clamp should receive the same treatment, since if the toolrest should move during the cutting it could foul the corners, and there would be a tendency for the wood to 'climb' over the toolrest, ripping itself from the mounting in the machine and creating a most dangerous situation. Sensible and methodical setting-up and checking will make the job safe.

Before describing the actual process of roughing down, there are two points which should be made clear concerning the way in which woodturning tools are held. Beginners who do not receive proper instruction will frequently fall into bad habits in this connection, in that they tend to grip the tool handles, and indeed the blades, far too fiercely, and to hold the blades in a manner which inhibits or even prohibits the free and fluid movement of the tool. The 'overhand' grip, with the fist wrapped round the blade and the back of the hand upward, is commonly used, and is undesirable. This is true of the 'under-hand' grip, with fist round the blade and back of the hand downward. Both these grips will prevent the free rolling and twisting movements of tools which are so vital to really good work, and they tend to be awkward in that parts of the lathe appear to be 'in the way'. The parts of the lathe are, of course, in the right place; it is the hand which is in the way. The grip I teach to my students facilitates tool manipulation and will not give rise to muscular pain, which is a curse to the 'death-grip' worker. The grip which I teach, and use myself for the vast majority of tool work, is one which I developed many years ago to suit myself, and which I refer to as the 'figure four'. It is best described as the placing of the first joint of the thumb across the second joint of the index finger at right-angles. The ball of the thumb holds the tool down on the toolrest and can help in moving the blade along, and the back of the index finger can be used to push the blade. It must be remembered that the hand which holds the handle, normally the dominant hand, does most of the work. The blade hand assists as required, particularly in the more intricate detail cuts.

There is no need for any particular problem to be experienced by left-handed workers as opposed to right-handed ones, since the lathe is not built specifically for either and it is necessary to be able to perform cuts in both left-to-right and right-to-left movements. It has been my experience, with more than three thousand students, that left-handed men and women manage perfectly well and do not feel any more awkward than right-handed students.

Roughing Down

The operation of roughing down is normally the first stage in the making of an item in the lathe, and is followed by roughing out. The roughing gouge is very useful indeed for such work, but inexperienced workers should be careful when using it in hollows as it can be quite vicious if wrongly presented. The virtue of a roughing gouge is that it removes wood very quickly, leaving a relatively poor finish which is acceptable because other tools will follow, taking cleaner cuts.

A piece of soft timber such as pine will do for the first attempt, about 3 inches square and 8 or 9 inches long. The speed should be one at which the operator feels comfortable, and this may well be about 1,500 rpm. It will be best to err on the slow side, since the exact speed is not important.

One of the most essential things for any beginner to comprehend is the vital importance of the angle of attack of the bevel to the surface of the timber when using a cutting tool. Good woodturners use a constant pressure with cutting tools, adjusting the depth of cut by a pivotal action of the bevel against the wood. The more the tool is 'tipped up' (angle of attack increased) the deeper it will cut if the pressure is maintained. The instinctive use of this pivotal action with the bevels takes some time and practice to acquire and perfect, but once it has become ingrained as a habit the quality of the work will be tremendously improved, and the bill for abrasive paper will be down to a fraction of its original size.

The reduction of a square to a cylinder by means of the roughing gouge is really a straightforward process, and the action of the tool is considerably smoother than most people expect. There is no dreadful bumping sensation, unless the heel of the gouge is striking the wood, which will mean that the handle is being held too low. This is most unlikely, since most people using this tool in the learning stages have exactly the opposite fault – they pull the handle up until the edge is being dragged in a scraping action across the timber. The handle of the gouge should be kept as low as possible, commensurate with the removal of a satisfactory amount of wood. It is important to bear in mind that properly presented edges remain sharp for quite long periods, whereas edges which are allowed to drag across the surface of the work in a scraping manner are quickly destroyed.

After sufficient practice it will become a simple matter to start at one end of the wood and pull the tool through to the other, repeating this procedure until a cylinder has been produced. Initially, however, it will be best to divide the job roughly into three parts, reducing the first two in one direction and the last one the other way. The cutting is a matter of holding the gouge firmly, but not tightly, and keeping the handle low. The tool must be placed on the toolrest before it touches the wood, then pushed forward until it begins to cut. Note that I have said 'pushed forward' rather than 'tipped up'. It is a common mistake among beginners to bring the edge on to the wood by tipping the tool up, which produces the wrong angle of attack. Because the tool must be pushed forward to the wood each time, it is vital that the blade be supported with the hand rather than gripped. A tight grip on to the blade of a cutting tool can prevent a student from making progress.

As we have seen, the reduction of the square to a cylinder will be effected by reducing three areas, two of which will be cut in one direction, the third the opposite way, so that no cuts run on to the end of the wood. These cuts are simple enough, since no manipulation is required. The tool is pushed forward until it is cutting, then traversed to left or right, but care must be taken to see that there is no swing of the blade. This simply means that both handle and blade must move at the same speed. If the blade moves fractionally faster, the cut will deteriorate as the cutting angle changes.

In any cut which is intended to travel along a straight surface and to remove a shaving of constant thickness, swinging of the blade must be avoided. Unfortunately this is a very common fault indeed with beginners, and stays with many people all their woodturning lives. It arises mainly because inexperienced turners want to stand close up to the work, whereas an experienced worker will stand back from it extending the arms so that cuts can be completed without any need to swing the blade or to move the feet.

In this operation, the first section should be brought to cylindrical form before starting on the next, and in the learning stage it may be found difficult to judge the exact moment when the last vestiges of the corners disappear. Rather than lightly touching the top of the rotating wood, as an experienced turner would do, it is better to stop the lathe to examine progress. Remember that tools should always be used with some pressure against the wood, and the temptation to stroke the surface lightly in order to achieve a 'light cut' must be resisted at all costs. This merely results in the removal of dust, and the rapid deterioration of the cutting edge. It is best from the very beginning to avoid the idea of 'light cuts', since this expression suggests light pressure with the tools. Firm pressure is required, and when I need to remove a shaving the thickness of a hair I will be applying more pressure, not less, so that I can achieve the requisite high degree of control. The concept of a *fine* cut, with pressure of the bevel against the wood, will be far more helpful when learning the craft.

Once this first piece of wood has been brought to a cylinder it can be used for further examination of the basic cuts, but the toolrest should first be moved in towards the wood, the effective diameter of which will now have been greatly reduced. Contrary to the advice given in some quarters, it is neither necessary nor desirable to position toolrests 'as close as possible' to the wood. Common sense should be used, the idea being to have the toolrest sensibly close to the wood, so that there is no excessive overhang of the tool which might make control difficult. A small gap between toolrest and wood will allow the shavings to escape while the tools are cutting, which is important for a beginner, who needs to watch the cut. If the gap is too small, shavings build up on the toolrest, obscuring the end of the gouge or chisel.

Smoothing and Planing

The roughing gouge, if sharp and correctly used, will produce reasonable surface finishes, but its function is the rapid removal of wood. Smoothing and planing of surfaces are operations which must be considered carefully. For the purposes of this book I am regarding a smoothing cut as one which improves a relatively rough surface, such as that left by a roughing gouge. A planing cut is one in which the tool works very much like a plane, in that

it will cut through any high spots on the wood in its first traverse, missing the low points, and after two or three cuts the surface will be smooth *and flat*.

At this stage we have arrived at one of the very important aspects of good tool work in woodturning, which must be fully appreciated by those who hope to become good at the craft. This is the absolute necessity for shearing cuts with sharp edges if first-class finishes are to be produced straight from the tools, with no requirement for abrasive paper. The importance of this cannot be too greatly emphasised, and I demonstrate the matter to students in my workshop by using a roughing gouge in an unusual manner to prove the point. When a roughing gouge has been used in the orthodox way, the surface will be reasonable, but by no means as smooth as that which would be produced by a correctly manipulated spindle gouge or skew chisel. Having produced a typical roughing gouge finish, I invite students to inspect it, then I cut again along part of the surface, with the gouge inverted on the toolrest, as shown in the sketch. The inversion of the blade

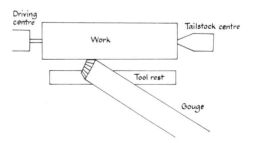

Here the gouge is completely inverted, its concave surface down to the toolrest, and the cutting is being done with a paring action, just short of the corner.

allows me to present the section of the edge which actually cuts at an oblique angle relative to the axis of the workpiece or to the toolrest. This provides a shearing cut instead of a cut which crosses the grain of the wood almost at right angles. This point will be referred to again later in the book, and is of paramount importance to those who wish to become better-than-average turners.

When the roughing gouge is used inverted, the corner is kept clear of the wood and the tool is moved steadily along the toolrest, bevel pressed against the work. The improvement in surface finish if this cut is correctly performed is little short of miraculous. The tool is not normally used in this way, but the demonstration shows my students that the same edge which has just roughed down a piece of wood can give a mirror-like finish when applied in a different manner. The whole point of the exercise is to demonstrate the fact that the edge of a cutting tool needs this slicing action if it is to produce the coveted smooth-surface finishes. The really effective use of spindle gouges and skew chisels is dependent upon this principle.

Mastery of a skew chisel without sound practical instruction is by no means easy, and unfortunately many people give the idea up after a succession of minor accidents. The important thing here is that skew chisels are not dangerous, but it is certainly much more difficult for anyone to teach himself or herself the use of a skew chisel than the use of a gouge. In other words it is not accurate to say that skews are dangerous, but it is certainly true to say that many people are dangerous when using them. The dig-in from a skew chisel is normally far more spectacular, and devastating to the nervous system, than that from a gouge, but such incidents can be avoided by obtaining some good practical tuition.

The approach to the use of a skew for smoothing is not complicated, and if the instructions given here are followed accurately there should be little trouble.

The smoothing cut is a finishing cut, and will produce the best results when a fine shaving is being removed. It is possible to cut heavily, and the performance can be quite impressive, but the surface of the wood will suffer, just as it does with a woodworker's plane which is set to take a heavy cut, because the material is being split away rather than peeled off. Remember that the object with cutting tools is always to remove wood without disturbing the fibres beneath it, which requires constant practice.

The following ten points are vital to good smoothing work with a skew chisel, and when things go wrong this list should be checked. It is almost certain that the problem will then be revealed.

1.   The area of the bevel which immediately surrounds the part of the edge which is cutting *must* rub the wood. If this is not the case, the finished surface will be smothered in tiny ridges, and the tool may well be difficult to control.

2.   Only the 'safe' area of the cutting edge can be allowed to contact the wood. This of course will be the section of the edge which is receiving direct support from the toolrest, as shown in the sketch. Any attempt to cut with the area which is shown unshaded will result in a dig-in.

3.   The angle of the cutting edge itself to the longitudinal axis of the work should be about 45 degrees.

4.   The toolrest should be raised so

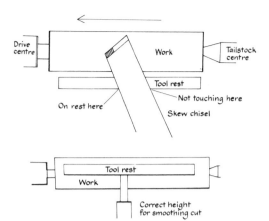

Smoothing cut with a skew chisel. Only the supported part of the edge can be used safely.

Plan view of smoothing operation with skew chisel. Only the shaded part of the blade can safely be used. Correct height of toolrest also shown.

that it is just below the top of the work-piece.

5. The tool must not be 'swung'. In other words, the hand which holds the handle must move at exactly the same speed as the one holding the blade, so maintaining the angle of the cutting edge at 45 degrees to the axis of the work.

6. The rate of feed, or speed of travel, of the tool along the toolrest must be kept to a minimum which will permit the whole surface of the wood to be cut. Moving too fast will produce spiral ridges.

7. The height of the cut, or distance of the cutting point forward from the edge of the toolrest, must remain con-stant. If it does not, the cut will become deeper and the tool will judder as the cutting point becomes lower.

8. Note that the edge of a skew chisel fades unusually quickly in this cut

which is not important in normal work as this is a finishing cut, and it will in most cases be performed once only, over a given surface. When practising, however, the tool will need to have its edge freshened on the grindstone fairly frequently.

9. The position of the turner relative to the lathe should be such as to permit the full movement to be made without movement of the feet.

10. The lower corner of the skew will not dig in if it touches the wood, in fact it has full support, but it should be kept clear of the wood because it will spoil the surface.

All this may seem very complicated, but with practice the movement will become instinctive, and once learned correctly this cut will never be forgotten. One problem which seems to worry numerous people is that the sharp edges of the sides of the chisels, being of hard steel, make small in-dentations in the surface of the toolrest, which can be a nuisance when trying to move tools smoothly. This can be rectified by filing the toolrest, which is of softer steel than the tools, but the best approach is to remove the sharp corners from the chisels by light treatment on the grinder.

The basis of the whole craft is the ability to execute the cuts described here, and sufficient practice will bring maximum safety and efficiency provided that the procedures are approached with a full and complete understanding of what is required. Safety for the worker, and for any onlookers, is of course of paramount importance, and efficiency is highly desirable if jobs are not to take far longer than they should. The use of abrasive paper will be comparatively rare in the case of a good turner, but is likely to take up much time in the case of a bad one. Deviation from the methods described here should not be undertaken until considerable practice has been put in and sufficient experience gained to permit sound judgement. Even then, such deviation is unwise unless the worker is entirely satisfied that the modified procedure will remain within the parameters of safety and efficiency.

CONVEX AND CONCAVE CURVES

The only components available to the woodturner when making shapes are concave curves, convex curves, and flat surfaces, and the most complex of projects can only contain these three forms. It is obvious, therefore, that the ability to produce perfect curves and flat surfaces must be the primary object of all beginners.

Perhaps the best way to approach the cutting of convex curves is by shaping the ends of a piece of wood 3 inches or so in diameter, endeavouring to create and maintain true curves with smooth surfaces straight from the gouge. A skew chisel could be used, but this is far more difficult

for novices, and it is worth noting that the rolling of a skew chisel round a ball is considered to be the most difficult of all the cuts. The shaping of curves such as those we are looking at here would also be a very much slower process if done with a chisel, so it is normally done with a spindle gouge, a skew being used for the final one or two cuts to improve the finish if this is felt necessary.

Many people believe that softwoods, such as pine, cannot be turned satisfactorily, but this is quite untrue. A skilled turner can produce a 'billiard-ball' finish with a gouge or chisel taken straight from the grinding wheel, even on soft timbers, a fact which I always demonstrate to my students. Such materials will, however, be found difficult to work in the early stages of learning the craft because their fibres are easily disturbed by poor cutting techniques. They do not suffer fools gladly, but for that very reason they are first class for practice purposes. It is also worth noting that well-turned pine artefacts will sell readily, and fetch relatively high prices, because so few people can produce them.

The tool which will be used for the shaping of curves, both convex and concave, is the spindle gouge, in this case the size of the tool will be a $\frac{1}{2}$-inch. Note that the sizes quoted for woodturning tools should be regarded as nominal. The width of a gouge is measured across the inside of the flute, or hollow area, and will usually be found to be slightly over or under the quoted size. This does not significantly affect the user.

Convex Curves

Practice on the convex curve can be started by roughing down a piece of wood between centres, and cleaning up the re-

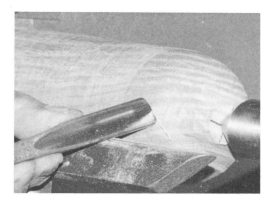

Convex curve cutting with a spindle gouge, using the supported part of the edge.

sulting rough cylindrical surface with a sharp skew chisel. The ½-inch spindle gouge, freshly sharpened, should have a profile similar to the shape of a man's fingernail. These tools must not be ground to a pointed shape, or they will be extremely difficult to control. The initial shaping of the end of the wood to a half-ball profile is not particularly difficult after a reasonable period of practice, but must be approached with an understanding of tool manipulation or the results will be poor. Depth of cut with cutting tools must always be a function of the angle of attack of the bevel to the surface of the work, not a matter of pushing harder to achieve a deeper cut. In fact, if a cut can be made deeper by adding pressure, the tool is being wrongly presented. In this cut there are four distinct movements which must be smoothly co-ordinated if the shape and finish are to be satisfactory. These movements are:

1. A lateral movement of the tool along the toolrest.
2. A forward movement of the tool as the diameter of the workpiece decreases.
3. A slight raising of the handle as the cut proceeds.
4. A 90-degree swing of the handle, to keep the bevel in contact with the wood and to maintain the depth of cut.

This may sound complex, but with practice these movements will become instinctive, and smooth co-ordination will be achieved. The making of the curve is commenced with the tool on the toolrest, tilted in the direction required, so that it is neither on its side nor on its back, but in a midway position between these two extremes. This, with the bevel correctly presented, will provide a shearing or slicing cut which is essential in order to produce the best quality finish. As the tool cuts, its corner must be kept just clear of the wood or smooth progress will be difficult and the surface will be ruined. Only the area of the cutting edge which is receiving direct support from the toolrest can safely be used, and in this case it will be the section of the edge immediately inside the flute and clear of the corner. This section must do the work throughout the cut; the remainder of the edge must be kept clear or the tool will either skid or dig in. If a multitude of rings and ridges should appear, this is a direct indication that the bevel is not rubbing on the wood under the shaving even though the turner may believe that it is.

Try working on the right-hand end of the wood for a start, beginning the cut an inch or so from the end and swinging the handle smoothly to the right to form a small curve. This can be enlarged by a series of similar cuts, starting a little further along the wood for each one, until the required 'quadrant' profile is achieved.

Note that as each cut nears its end there will be a problem, in that a point will be reached where it is impossible to proceed without pushing the corner of the tool into the waste wood. At this point the tool is rolled smoothly to the right so that the cut is completed with the exact centre of its edge. Try this with the lathe switched off, moving the tool round slowly so that you can study the movement, and don't be discouraged if it takes a while to get the feel of the thing.

When making convex curves which are intended to flow from a straight surface, a common error is to push the tool *into* the wood at the start of the cut. This immediately produces a reduction in diameter, or 'step', which is undesirable and difficult to remove. The cut should start with insufficient angle of attack, in other words the handle of the tool should be too far back away from the end of the wood to permit the edge to cut. It is allowed to rub the wood, and the handle is swung to increase the angle of attack of the bevel to the wood. When the cut starts, the movement of the tool round the curve can begin. This method ensures a smooth flow with no sign of the dreaded 'step'.

When convex curves of this type can be made smoothly and efficiently, a skew chisel can be used to impart an extra-fine finish, but it must be used in the same way as was described for smoothing on a straight surface, its edge slicing a shaving away. The problem here is that the bevel must still remain in firm contact with the wood immediately below the shaving, and the cut must remain entirely within the safe area of the blade. It is not an easy cut, and the dig-in which can result from it is quite dramatic. It is best left until all other cuts have become second nature.

Rounding over of the left-hand end of the work is done in the same manner, but obviously in the reverse direction. There is no need to reverse the hands on the tool or to change the attitude of the body to the lathe, but it is necessary to ensure that the swing of the tool can be completed without obstruction. In other words, it will be necessary to stand back from the lathe and extend the arms so that the handle can be swung without hindrance.

Concave Curves

Concave curves also require considerable manipulation of the gouge during the cut, and they present certain problems for beginners. These problems are evident on every woodturning course in my workshop, and if they can be explained fully to the students, success becomes truly a measure of effort. The real trouble with all these manipulative cuts, where both an exact shape and a high-quality finish are required, is that there seems to be far too much to think about. This is all part of

Shaping a concave form with a spindle gouge. Shaving leaves the edge just inside the supported corner.

the experience of entering into a new activity where complex skills are needed and should not be allowed to depress the novice, who will find that given initial understanding, practice is the answer.

Once again, a 3-inch square piece of wood – softwood will do very well – can be roughed down to a cylinder and cleaned up neatly with a couple of cuts from a sharp skew chisel. For practice purposes, these workpieces may be kept at a length which is a little shorter than that of the toolrest, so that there is no need for work to be interrupted while the toolrest is moved about. Concave-curve cutting is best approached by cutting large coves, which for present purposes can be regarded as symmetrical hollows into which a circular shape could be partly fitted. The curve of the shape must be constant throughout, with no sudden changes of direction. That is the ultimate aim, but this is one of the most difficult cuts if it is done correctly so that both the final shape and finish are of high quality. It is an easy cut if it is done almost correctly, near-success being within the capabilities of any beginner. Strong self-criticism is called for here, and the 'near enough' approach just will not do.

The action required is a scooping one, and there is a bonus for the beginner in that the movement of the tool is identical to that employed in hollowing a bowl. The novice who has conquered this cut between centres will therefore have a distinct advantage when the time comes to start on bowl-turning. The gouge used on a bowl will be different, but the movement is the same.

The rules of woodturning state that all cuts must be made 'downhill', from a larger diameter towards a smaller, so shapes of this nature are made by cutting from

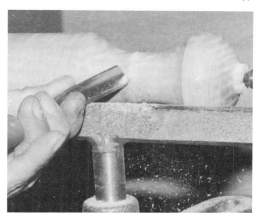

Practice is needed to enable left and right cuts to meet correctly.

the outside of the hollow towards the centre, and in order to keep the shape in balance throughout the cutting it is best to cut alternately from each side. The operation is begun by making a small hollow at the centre of the length of wood and enlarging this by successive cuts until both shape and desired size are satisfactory. It is important to remember that the corners of the gouge must be kept clear of the wood and that the centre of the edge is not used, therefore the cutting sections of the edge lie to left and right of the central point, stopping just short of the corners. The part of the edge which is cutting should be presented so that it can slice the wood, which means that the tool is halfway between being fully on its side or fully on its back. The handle is swung backwards during the cut as the edge moves along the wood, this backward movement of the handle being vital, since it 'draws' the shape. A common fault is in making too little handle movement, which results in a torn surface and a shape which is nothing like the required curve.

One of the most irritating aspects, where beginners are concerned, is the frequent skidding of the tool as an attempt is made to start the cut. This is unlikely to injure the worker, but the problem must be overcome before actual projects are undertaken or many of them will be ruined. When a gouge skids in this manner, it produces a nasty spiral tear in the wood. The usual cause of this phenomenon is that the handle of the gouge is being held too high, which can be proven by experimenting while the lathe is switched off, the wood being rotated slowly by hand. (This system is always useful when trying to establish the cause of a skid or dig-in with any tool.) Place the gouge in position for starting the cut, turn the wood slowly by hand, and contact the wood with the handle held too low, so that the heel of the bevel contacts the wood. In this position the angle of attack of bevel to wood is insufficient, and the tool cannot cut. Keep the wood moving while increasing the angle of attack until a shaving begins to curl away from the cutting edge. This is the correct starting position, and should be committed to memory. Now continue to increase the angle of attack slowly, still rotating the wood, and you will soon find the gouge skidding slowly back along the surface of the timber. This sort of 'post mortem' on skids and dig-ins can be invaluable.

It is important when cutting with chisels and gouges to keep some pressure against the wood with the bevel, and to be quite certain that the edge is not being dragged along the wood with no bevel support. Remember that it should be impossible to produce a thicker shaving by pressing harder, since depth of cut is a direct function of angle of attack of bevel to timber. If pressure is used, and the cut is being performed correctly, there will be a bonus in that the bevel will polish the surface which is revealed as the shaving is removed.

After sufficient practice, which may be over quite a long period, it will be possible to achieve near-perfect results in this operation, so that the last two cuts are continuous down each side of the shape and leave no rings or roughness to show where they met. A shape of this kind could of course be made with a round-nosed scraper, and sanded smooth. Such an approach, however, would certainly not satisfy anyone who really wanted to become a woodturner.

BEADS

Another basic cut is the bead, which is very difficult to describe without the resulting explanation sounding extremely complicated. In fact, the thing is a knack which is not too hard to acquire, provided the initial approach is sound. My analysis of the bead cut is in the form of a five-point formula which has become well known around the world, and I find that since I produced it the teaching of bead-cutting in my workshop has become much easier. The point, or 'long corner', of a skew chisel is used for bead-cutting, and the five points are:

1.   On the toolrest
2.   Off at the back
3.   Edge square
4.   *Find* the height
5.   Along and round

Naturally most people are aware that the tool goes on the toolrest, but point 1 means that as the tool is placed there, the turner mentally notes that contact between tool and toolrest must not be broken until the cut is complete. Concentration will be upon the point of the tool, since this is the only part that cuts – none of the actual edge is involved. It is quite easy to pivot the tool on the wood, raising the handle, until the tool is actually *off* the toolrest, and the wood will soon put it back with some violence.

The back of a skew chisel, for the purposes of bead cutting, is the shorter of the two sides, which should be raised by about the thickness of a playing card from the toolrest. If this raising is overdone the shaping of the bead will be difficult or impossible. If the tool is not lifted off at all, then *all* its edge will cut, which is quite obviously undesirable.

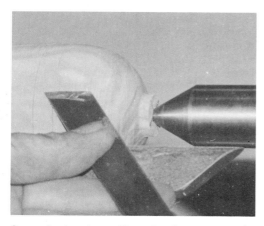

Start of a bead cut. The edge is square to the marked line, and the right-hand side of the chisel is just clear of the toolrest.

Before commencing the cutting of a bead it is usual to mark out its width, and most workers do this with the point of the chisel, making two faint lines. Point 3 is a reference to the fact that as the cut commences, the cutting edge of the chisel should be parallel to the toolrest, or in other words square to these lines.

Point 4 is the most important, since if it is not understood and observed there is almost no hope of anything resembling a bead. The height in question is that of the point of the chisel above the toolrest, which needs to be such as to permit the point to enter the wood without any of the edge becoming involved. The procedure for establishing this height exactly is not difficult once it is understood, but it must be quite clear to the student that an incorrect height will result in an incorrect shape. To find the height it is necessary to position the tool in accordance with the first three points, and to bring it into contact with the surface of the wood at a height which is slightly excessive, so that the point cannot enter the wood. If the tool is now pulled back and brought down the wood until its point describes a very faint scratch line, the height has been established. Under no circumstances should the tool be brought any lower, or too much wood will be cut away and the shape of the bead will be wrong. To ensure accuracy in this it is necessary to have the chisel rubbing against the wood as it is brought back to find the height, and the noise produced by its rubbing will be clearly audible. The blade must not be twisted to bring its point into contact with the wood. This action will eventually cause the chisel to scratch the wood, but not at the correct height. No twisting of the tool should occur until the height has been accurately established.

The point of the chisel, once the first four points have been attended to, will do the cutting, starting very close to the centre of the area marked out for the bead. Point 5 is intended to indicate that the tool must be moved along as it is rolled over,

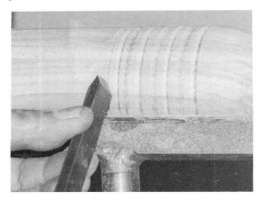

Beads require plenty of practice. Note the finishing position of the skew, fully on its side and square to the toolrest.

or it will not reach the marked line and the size of the bead will be wrong. As the cut is made, the tool is rolled over and the handle is swung to move in the same direction as the chisel point, so that the position of the chisel at the end of the cut will be completely on its side, handle square to the toolrest. Failure to complete the movement is a common fault among my students, but unless the full movement

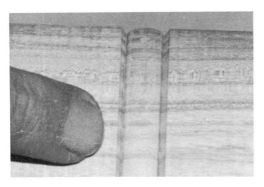

Bead cut with a skew chisel point. Note that the edges have been trimmed to remove 'whiskers'.

is made the full shape of the bead will not be produced.

The most likely problems for beginners here are lifting the tool off the toolrest while cutting, which results in a ruined bead and possibly a dig-in; holding both blade and handle of tool much too tightly; and allowing the tool to move down the wood during the cut instead of maintaining the carefully selected height. Lots of practice is called for, and I tell my students that the first five thousand beads are the worst – after that it's all downhill.

TRIMMING WITH SKEW CHISEL POINT

The point of a skew chisel is of great value to a woodturner, since it produces all those beautifully clean and crisp detail sections which make his work stand out far above that produced by the uninitiated. It is, however, necessary to bear in mind that the chisel point is a fragile thing, so examine it carefully prior to any attempt at fine detail cutting. The problem is that the point has only to catch against another tool on the bench, or be knocked lightly against the lathe, to lose its cutting ability. Always give a chisel a rub on the grinder before attempting fine work.

While still considering chisel-point work it may be as well to look at a cut which always forms part of my woodturning courses, since there is a high element of potential danger involved if the procedure is not fully comprehended. This is the use of a skew chisel point for the trimming of end grain, and the cut is extremely useful. The danger to which I refer is that of a violent dig-in, which has been known to cause serious injuries. This is not in any way intended to put beginners off, in fact quite the reverse. The cut is easy to perform, and there is very little chance of any problem once the matter has been fully explained.

If the end of a piece of wood is trimmed with a parting tool to bring the job to a given length, which is a common operation, the resulting finish will be very poor by the standards of an experienced turner.

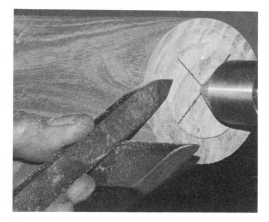

Trimming to length with a parting tool. The handle is raised slowly as the cut proceeds.

The surface can be immensely improved by cutting across it with the chisel point, a procedure which calls for understanding rather than skill. When the chisel is used in this way on pine or other softwoods, the surface produced will be very good indeed. When close-grained hardwoods are cut in this manner, the finish can be like glass. A point of interest here is that parting tools are very easy to use, but it is as well to note that any tool which is easy to use in this craft will produce poor surfaces. The cutting action of the parting tool in the cut under discussion is quite different from that of the chisel, and the

use of the skew chisel point in this cut has a fundamental principle which is inherent in *all* chisel-point work. If we recall the three rules which I gave earlier (see page 20), it will be noted that my own rule states that 'only that part of any cutting edge which is receiving direct support from the toolrest can safely be used'. In this particular case, the part of the cutting edge used is at the extreme point, which has full support from the toolrest since the tool is in a 'long corner down' position.

A simple way to discover what lies behind all this is to return to our analytical approach of turning the workpiece slowly by hand, with the lathe switched off and with the chisel on the toolrest with its long corner down, bring the point into contact with the end of the wood. This will not produce any sign of misbehaviour or digging-in. If the tool is now twisted so that all its edge is on the end of the wood, it will snatch and roll into the timber. This is because direct support is available only

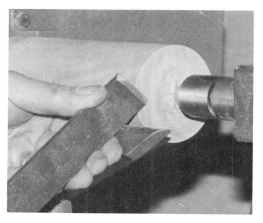

Trimming the end grain of a cylinder with the point of a skew chisel. Only the point can safely contact the wood.

at the extreme point, and little imagination is required to visualise the effect with the lathe running. The heart of all this is that in *all* chisel-point work only the point can be allowed to touch the wood.

To sum this up, it is perfectly in order to cut across the end of the wood to the centre with the point of a skew if *only* the point is permitted to make contact, the rest of the cutting edge leaning slightly away. The kind of dig-in which can result from faulty technique in this sort of work is dangerous and traumatic in the extreme, and since it is all over in a second, those who experience it while trying to teach themselves are unable to learn from their mistakes.

One last point on this. When cutting across the end of a workpiece in this manner, the point of the chisel should travel towards the centre of the wood, so there is a slight raising of the handle.

5 Basic Faceplate Work

The term 'faceplate work' is used in a general sense among woodturners, and does not necessarily refer to work which is held on a faceplate. It may do, but the expression is a general reference to work which is supported at the headstock only, the tailstock not being used. The lathe accessory which actually holds the workpiece may be a faceplate, but it is just as likely to be some form of chuck and, due to the tremendous rise in interest in this craft over the past ten years or so, there is now a very wide variety of chucks available. In some ways this is a good thing, but the situation is confusing to anyone setting out to learn the craft, and unless considerable care is taken it is very easy to waste money on gadgetry which is produced to make a profit for the manufacturer rather than to be of positive help to the turner.

FACEPLATES

In this chapter we are looking at some of the devices used to secure workpieces when the tailstock is not used, and there are quite a few of them. Faceplates as such are very simple devices, being little more than discs of metal, drilled and countersunk so that screws can be put through from the back of the plate into the timber.

The faceplate is threaded so that it can be screwed on to the mandrel of the lathe, and usually has a wide rim which helps to stiffen it. Unfortunately many manufacturers now make faceplates from some kind of aluminium alloy, which is not as good for the purpose as steel. The problem is that many turners who are not aware of the inherent snag will screw the faceplate very firmly to blanks of timber which are not flat, and the cheaper forms of faceplate are quickly distorted. It is always advisable to plane a blank truly flat on the side which is to go against the faceplate, and better still to pass the wood through a thicknesser, so that both faces are flat and parallel. Another annoying point is that most manufacturers of lathes supply a faceplate which is 7 or 8 inches

Avon faceplate attached to a large walnut bowl blank by means of three screws.

53

in diameter, and many do not offer a smaller one even as an optional extra. There is no harm in having a faceplate of this size, but a smaller one, say about 4½ or 5 inches in diameter, is really worthwhile. The Avon lathes score heavily here, since they offer a small faceplate which is beautifully engineered from steel.

The turning of bowls and dishes, together with such items as bases for standard lamps, is the area in which faceplates are most used. The larger the disc, of course, the larger the size of faceplate used, to bring support for the wood out near the edge. When we discuss the subject of bowl-turning, however, it will be seen that a small faceplate can sometimes be a real blessing.

CHUCKS

When I took up the craft, back in 1944, there were few lathe manufacturers and even fewer items of ancillary equipment for lathes. In those days one relied upon faceplates, woodscrew chucks, and various home-made chucks for specific operations. Today's beginner is faced with a choice of chucks and other optional equipment which is quite bewildering. The thing to remember is that none of us needs every item of equipment currently being offered, and some time spent in ensuring that what is purchased is likely to be useful will be well spent. It is still possible to make wooden devices to hold wood for specific operations, and some are shown here. Many of the chucks advertised now are expensive, and some are not as brilliant as the advertisements would have us believe, and my advice to beginners is that they should buy items of this kind only

when they have established beyond doubt that they are necessary.

Woodscrew Chuck

Woodscrew chucks are still well worth having, though many novices are rather diffident about using them because the retaining screws are into the end grain of the timber, and a dig-in can rip the work from the chuck. The answer to this is to learn woodturning properly, and to practise until sufficient competence is achieved before going on to chuck work. The grip offered by a screw chuck, even the smaller versions which use only one screw, is a great deal firmer than many people think, provided that the wood has been put on to the chuck correctly. I use both the large and small types a great deal, and find them excellent for a wide variety of operations. They are normally available in two sizes, 1½ inch and 2½ inch. These are measurements across the faces of the chucks. The smaller one has one screw only, at its centre, and is very useful for egg cups, cupboard knobs, chessmen, small finials and many other items where a larger chuck might obstruct the movement of the cutting tool. The bigger version has provision for extra screws around the outer part of its face, giving greater support for the blank. I use this one for bowls up to about 8 inches in diameter, and in many other jobs, such as the turning of tankards, large goblets and the like. Good woodscrew chucks have central screws which are replaceable, and this should be checked before buying one, since if the screw cannot be replaced there will be a big problem as soon as it is worn or has been chewed up by a parting tool. In the early stages of learning chuck work it is advisable not to attempt the turning of

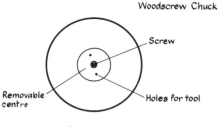

Woodscrew Chuck

Screw

Removable
centre

Holes for tool

Front view

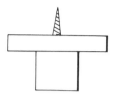

Side view

Face of Coronet woodscrew chuck, showing replaceable screw in centre. Two holes in the disc which retains the screw permit its removal with a special tool.

Coronet woodscrew chuck fitted to an Avon lathe by means of an adaptor.

blanks more than about 3 inches long on the smaller woodscrew chucks, since there is quite a lot of leverage exerted when cut-

ting on the end farthest from the chuck, and the job may become loose or even knocked from its mounting.

Engineer's Chuck

One type of chuck which should be avoided is known as an 'engineer's chuck', and this is the most expensive type likely to be found among the advertisements.

Engineer's chuck: not recommended for use in woodturning.

These items are very large and heavy, can be extremely dangerous when used on wood lathes, and are horrendously expensive. They are used a great deal in metal-turning, where they are efficient, but they are designed to hold metal, not wood. The point here is that their jaws can be tightened up on a piece of metal, and will hold firmly, whereas the more they are tightened on to wood, the more the wood is compressed, and so the job is never really secure. In addition to this, these chucks have four sets of jagged jaws which protrude from the sides. In metal-work the speeds of rotation are much lower than in woodturning, but at woodturning speeds the jaws are invisible, and unless special precautions are taken, serious hand injury can result.

Jacobs Pattern Chuck

Woodturners use the three-jawed Jacobs pattern chuck, which has a tapered shank to fit into either headstock or tailstock as the occasion demands, and this can be very useful for drilling or for holding sanders and the like. Note, however, that when used without end pressure, such as would be present when drilling, there is no positive location for the chuck in the machine.

Jacobs pattern chuck with Morse tapered shank for use in headstock or tailstock. A variety of drill bits can be used.

In such situations, when using sanders for example, the tailstock should be brought up so that its centre is just touching the sander, so preventing the chuck from working loose.

Collet Chuck

A collet chuck is one which closes as it is tightened, so providing a firm grip on whatever is placed in its jaws. Typical

examples of this variety are to be found on electric drills or routers. A home-made wooden collet chuck is illustrated, and will work very well on many jobs, but there are now some nicely engineered metal examples which are efficient but which normally form part of a composite metal 'chucking system'. This sort of thing is usually offered for sale as a 'three-in-one chuck', a 'six-in-one chuck' or whatever the case may be. There are virtues in these

Collet chuck. The unit on the right fits inside the centre unit, and closes as the ring (*left*) is screwed home.

A partly completed chess pawn in a collet chuck.

Split Collet chuck

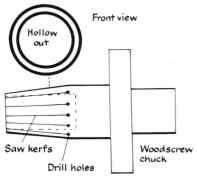

Front view

Hollow out

Saw kerfs

Drill holes

Woodscrew chuck

Split wooden chuck, home-made. The saw cuts run into pre-drilled holes to prevent splitting. Wood is turned with spigot to fit in chuck, and metal ring is tapped up taper to provide grip.

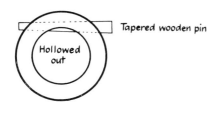

Tapered wooden pin

Hollowed out

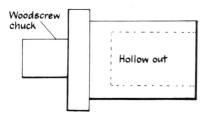

Woodscrew chuck

Hollow out

Collet chuck, home-made. Chuck is hollowed out as shown, and a tapered wooden pin is driven in to engage with a flat on the work.

multi-purpose devices, but most purchasers will find that they end up using them for only two or three operations.

Combination Chuck

Most 'combination chucks' currently available on the British market include collet facilities in a range of sizes, and once these have been used for a while they are likely to prove almost indispensable, though the home-made one illustrated on this page will do very well for most jobs. The collet chuck can be used to hold small cylindrical stock, which will be gripped very firmly, as in the making of knobs for furniture, or chessmen; I find them excellent when making chimneys, whistles, and other small parts for toy railway engines. It is worth pointing out, however, that while blanks which are larger in diameter than the capacity of the chuck can be dealt with, it is necessary to turn the wood to a cylinder between centres and to cut a pin at one end to fit into the collet chuck. Experience will show how long a piece of wood can safely or effectively be turned in this way, and it is best not to be too ambitious in this respect at first.

Some of the other components of these multi-purpose chucks are interesting, though their value will depend upon the interests of the individual turner to a large extent. The combination chuck itself consists of a body which screws on to the lathe mandrel, and a ring which screws over the nose of the chuck to retain and operate whatever is fitted at the time. The ring is normally provided with a hole in its periphery into which a special spanner can be fitted. These devices are not cheap, and the purchase of a combination chuck should be given some careful thought, but many turners do find them extremely useful.

A combination chuck as supplied by Tyme Machines of Bristol, for their Avon and Cub lathes, is shown in the illustrations, but space will not permit a really

Multi-purpose chuck. These have become very popular in recent years.

thorough discussion of the full range of work which can be covered. One of the best advances in recent years has been the introduction of the *expanding* collet chuck to the range of equipment offered by retailers. These are, in my view, among the most useful items a beginner can acquire, though the manner in which they operate does cause some apprehension among those who have never used them. The essential difference between this type and the normal collet chuck is that they expand rather than contract when tightened. Possibly the best way to explain this will be to look at the turning of a wooden plate, which was always an awkward job because the plate needs to be turned fairly thin and the holding screws employed when using

Universal chuck assembled for expanding collet work. Note the special spanner for tightening.

a faceplate are not practical. The turning of plates was usually done by means of a recessed disc of scrap timber, referred to as a 'hollow wooden chuck', which I will return to later. The procedure when using the expanding collet chuck is simple, and a great deal quicker than other methods, but in addition it is extremely effective and the appearance of the finished plate or dish is improved by the system. I will explain the meaning of that comment in a moment.

When an expanding collet chuck is to be used, the disc of wood for the plate is mounted on a faceplate in the usual way, using four short screws, and the back, or underside, of the plate is shaped. When this has been done, a circular recess is cut at the centre of the job, using a sharp parting tool, to a depth of about an ⅛ inch, or even slightly less, and of a size to suit the particular chuck. At this point the job can, if desired, be sanded (as most discs must be), sealed with sanding sealer, and polished. The partly completed plate can now be removed from the faceplate, and the chuck can be fitted to the shallow recess and tightened firmly with the special spanner. Examination of these chucks will reveal that their jaws are dovetail shaped, and some people undercut the edge of the recess with the point of a skew chisel to accept the chuck jaws. I have not found this to be necessary, as the jaws cut into the wood when the chuck is tightened, and the grip on the job is surprisingly effective. Workpieces do not fly from these chucks, unless of course they have been improperly mounted in the first place, and since there are no screws to worry about the plates can be turned as thin as required. The holes made by the original screws used in the faceplate mounting are turned out as the front, or upper side, of the plate is shaped. Naturally there are other items which can be turned on these devices, but a plate provides the best example of its application.

Pin Chuck

One type of chuck which forms part of some universal chuck systems is the pin chuck. This is a fairly recent arrival on the woodturning scene. It is one of those items of equipment which will be a tremendous asset to some workers and may hardly ever be used by others. It is suitable for a fairly small range of operations, for which it is excellent. A pin chuck is cylindrical, 2 to 3 inches in length, with a flange at one end to permit its mounting in the combination chuck. The other end is tapered internally, but the significant thing is that an inclined plane is cut into the cylindrical surface. When the pin chuck has been mounted on the lathe the workpiece is drilled with a suitable hole, a short length of round steel (the 'pin') is laid in the inclined plane, and the blank to be turned is pushed on to the chuck. If the hole has been drilled correctly it will slide on easily. The principle involved is similar to that employed in the seat-belts of cars. When the lathe is stationary, the blank can be rotated by hand on the chuck in one direction, but not in the other, because the pin jams it. Once the lathe is started, the job is held very firmly by this pin, but when the job is finished it can be slid straight off the chuck. Various diameters of pin chuck are available, and workers will find their own uses for them, but obvious projects are pepper and salt pots or napkin rings. Curiously enough, pin chucks are also useful in bowl-turning.

The turning of bowls will be dealt with more fully later, but the system now

Square blocks for napkin rings are mounted as shown here. Pin chucks are also useful for salt or pepper pots.

A square block of wood has been mounted on a pin chuck and roughed down.

widely adopted by many woodturners is to cut the bowl blank to a circle on the band-saw, and to drill a hole at the centre for a pin chuck. The *outside* of the bowl is then shaped, and when this has been done the job can either be prepared for mounting on an expanding collet chuck, or reversed

on to a faceplate. The main problem with pin chucks is that they are unsuitable for many jobs because they would leave a hole. Another point worth noting, since the workshop of a busy turner is usually a mass of shavings, is that when removing a job from one of these chucks, care must be taken to see that the pin does not drop out. If it does, it may perhaps be recovered with the aid of a magnet, but if this fails a short length of a round nail will serve as a replacement.

One final point about these chucks which may interest a number of beginners is that, as I mentioned earlier, they are tapered internally. This means that small square lengths of wood can be inserted into them, and the tailstock brought up to apply pressure and to support the other end. This can be useful on fine work of any kind, but specifically on lace bobbins. In the past few years there has been a tremendous upsurge of interest in these artefacts, in fact almost all the students who come to me now seem to have the intention of making them in quantities. For those who have not encountered lace bobbins, I will merely state that they are

Lace bobbin chuck for Avon lathe. A small square blank is inserted and the tailstock supports the other end.

small decorated sticks, often with a ring of wire at one end on which beads are strung, and their true purpose is to give some tension to the threads when making lace. It now appears that most of them are in fact bought by collectors. They are fiddly little things to make, and I would be surprised if anyone made a fortune at it, but they are finely detailed and very demanding if turned well. Small bundles of blanks especially for lace bobbins are now offered for sale, though why people can't cut their own is a mystery. A lace bobbin blank is a short piece of square wood and is very thin, so that driving it by means of a normal drive centre can present problems. If the internal taper of a pin chuck is used, these problems are overcome. Note, however, that there will be a waste piece at each end which is cut off after the job is finished.

Home-made Chucks

There are numerous chucks which were at one time made by woodturners from scrap material, and they worked very well indeed, but many of these are now available as manufactured items in metal. The types of chuck chosen by a woodturner will depend upon the type of turning undertaken and, once the initial learning stages have been passed, most people seem to specialise to some extent. The best approach now may be to make up wooden chucks for jobs which are unlikely to be undertaken frequently, and to purchase the manufactured ones to be used on jobs which occur regularly. One simple device, which hardly merits the label 'chuck', is the recessed disc or block. These can be made from scrap hardwood or softwood, mounted on a woodscrew chuck or faceplate, a recess being cut in the face of the timber by means of a parting tool. This sort of holding device has its uses in bowl-turning, and is often employed when making wooden rings or circular picture frames. The recess has to be turned so that the workpiece is a good firm drive fit. If the fit is too slack the situation can be improved by thoroughly wetting the chuck with water, making the wood swell. An alternative is to place a sheet of brown paper across the front of the chuck before driving the workpiece in. This sort of chuck should have a hole 1 inch or so in diameter bored through its centre before it is used, so that when the job is completed a wooden rod can be passed through the hole and tapped with a mallet to dislodge the work. Sometimes the fit is really tight, and it could otherwise be difficult to remove the finished turning without damaging it.

6 Napkin Rings and Stands

A book which sets out to guide beginners in the craft of woodturning can become quite boring if no practical work is included, so as we move through some of the facets of turning, we can look at the making of a few items, which will help with the explanations of theory. I would emphasise that as much practice as possible should be done with work between centres before actual projects are undertaken, but having made that point I will now discuss the making of a set of napkin rings, together with a suitable stand on which they can be kept when not in use. Napkin rings sell quite well in sets, and make excellent gifts for family and friends. A close-grained hardwood is best, and one which has some interesting grain or colour will be a good choice. I am thinking of yew, which has both in abundance. Very nice napkin rings can be made from sections of yew branchwood, since the making of the rings removes the heart from the blank, and they are able to finish their drying evenly because the walls are thin. Like many operations in woodturning, there are several approaches, all of which have their merits, but the one I am outlining here is interesting. Those who have pin chucks of a suitable size will find them excellent, but I am using a wooden 'mandrel', which is an old method, once very much favoured.

Making the Rings

Some workers make these rings on a woodscrew chuck, using a short length of wood. This is hollowed out, initially by drilling, then by enlarging the hole with a parting tool or square-ended scraper, and finally, after the outside of the ring has been shaped, the finishing work is done and the ring is parted off from the rest of the blank, which is waste. There are, to my mind, three problems in this. It is not easy to ensure that the inside face of the ring is exactly parallel to the outside, it is difficult to get the inside really smooth, and the process of parting off can spoil the ring by tearing the wood as the tool breaks through.

The method described here may appear to be more trouble, but it will get round the problems I have mentioned and it can work really well if done with care. The material required will be a 2-inch square piece of wood about 8 inches long; four blocks, each 2 inches square; and a square piece of wood roughly 1 inch thick from which a disc about 4 inches in diameter can be cut.

The blocks are first drilled through with a $1\frac{1}{2}$-inch drill, into the end grain. Whatever type of drill bit is employed it must be really sharp and run at its correct speed, and the job is best done with a drill press. If this is not available, the blanks can be held in a vice and drilled with an electric drill or handbrace. If a 'flat bit' or 'spade bit' is used, this must be run at high speed, and when it has passed through the block the drill should be switched off before the bit is withdrawn. If this is not done the block may be damaged, because these drills are guided and steadied by their point, so if they are withdrawn from the wood while still rotating they tend to flap slightly and tear the wood. Centre these drilled holes exactly, and have a piece of scrap wood under the block so that the cutter can break through without damage. When the blocks have all been drilled (pessimists will make an extra one in case of accidents later) they can be set aside. The next step is to turn up a square length of wood to form a mandrel, which simply means mounting it between centres, running it down to a cylinder, and putting a slight taper on it, using a roughing gouge. There is no need to make the surface smooth, indeed it will be best to leave it rough to give a better grip for the square blanks. These are mounted, one at a time, by sliding them on to the mandrel and tapping them along until they are tightly gripped by the taper – and some experimenting may be needed to get the taper just right.

When one block is firmly in place and the tailstock has been tightened up on to the mandrel, the first ring can be made.

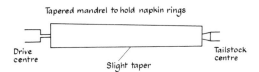

Mandrel with slight taper is turned from softwood to hold napkin ring blanks.

Use a roughing gouge, freshly ground, and work gently so that the grip of the mandrel is not loosened. When the blank is cylindrical the rest of the shaping can be done, using a sharp $\frac{1}{2}$-inch spindle gouge, and employing the correct slicing action. Any detail required will be put in with the point of the skew chisel, and those who have by now perfected their bead-cutting may like to put a small example of a bead at each end. Try not to get carried away by your artistic muse on this first ring, remember that the others will have to be exact copies, and copy turning is not easy. The motto here is 'keep it simple'.

When the outside of the ring is finished it can, if necessary, be sanded with fine paper, and when all four are completed in this way they can be put aside for a while. It is worth marking the mandrel clearly to show what it is, and drilling through one end of it so that it can be hung on the wall somewhere for future use. A block of scrap wood is now mounted on a woodscrew chuck, and the size of this block is not critical, it just has to be large enough to be hollowed out so that the rings can be pushed in. This is a version of the 'hollow wooden chuck' so often referred to in magazine articles.

The idea now is to make a hole in this block into which the rings can be fitted so that their inside faces can be sanded and/or polished as required, so care is needed in the hollowing to make sure that the fit will be good, and a *very* slight taper will help. As with most of these chucks, if the fit is a little slack, some brown paper will help. This whole operation is really a great deal easier than it sounds.

Making the Stand

When all four rings have been dealt with, the stand can be made, and this is a nice combination of disc- and stick-turning, which will provide very good experience. The more the subject of woodturning is discussed, the more obvious becomes the fact that a woodturner's shop is not complete without a good bandsaw, and I consider this tool sufficiently important to merit a short section later in the book. Poor bandsaws are more trouble than they are worth, and can cost their owners a small fortune in broken blades. If no bandsaw is available, the disc can be cut out with a coping saw, after it has been marked out with a pair of dividers so that its centre is clear. I normally use the larger of the woodscrew chucks for this job, using the central screw only, and it will not matter if the screw comes through the wood since the hole it makes will be hidden by the vertical part of the stand. Speed of rotation, as I pointed out earlier, is not critical, so run the lathe at a speed which suits you, and true up the outside edge of the disc first. This could be done with a sharp scraper, but a $\frac{3}{8}$-inch deep-fluted gouge will do a far better job. A little shaping can be done – a slight taper, or perhaps a gentle curve.

There is an important point of safety here which must not be overlooked, in that a dig-in on the edge of a disc can be very dangerous, so the angle of attack of the bevel to the wood must be kept as low as is possible commensurate with the removal of a shaving. If the bevel is rubbing correctly all will be well, but the turner's head should not be in line with the work.

The shaping of the face of the job can be undertaken next, with the toolrest moved round so that it runs across the workpiece, and set correctly in height so that with the bevel rubbing and the tool contacting the toolrest, the cut can travel to the exact centre. Any shape that pleases will do, but in these early days do try to resist the temptation to make detailed and difficult ones.

Either before or after the shaping, a hole must be made at the centre of the disc to accept the vertical part of the stand. Vertical units in jobs of this nature should always be located in this way, since the finished article will be strong, and there will be no question of the vertical part being off-centre. A popular method of producing such holes is to set up a Jacobs pattern chuck in the tailstock, fitted with a 1-inch drill bit, and position this close to the work. With the lathe running, the drill bit can be advanced safely and easily into the wood by means of the tailstock handwheel. I would use this method if I had a large number of discs to drill, but for one shallow recess like this it seems hardly worth the bother. The same effect can be achieved by marking out the area to be recessed and using a parting tool, starting at the outer edge of the area and making successive cuts until the centre is reached. Be careful not to cut the retaining screw. Any damage occasioned by such an error would be easily repaired in the case of the parting tool, but if the screw is damaged it will have to be replaced, and with some chucks this is a time-consuming operation.

A section dealing with polishing, and finishing in general, will be found elsewhere in the book, so I will not confuse the issue by describing it here, but the base of the stand is now completed, and can be put aside while the vertical section is turned. This is a straightforward piece of spindle-turning, and should be well within the capabilities of those who have been practising the cuts described in the earlier chapters. It is a typical piece of spindle-turning, so the roughing gouge can be used to bring the job to a cylinder which will accept the rings as a comfortable sliding fit, putting a bit of shape into the part which is visible when the rings are in place. Jobs of this kind usually have a waste piece left at the tailstock end which is removed with a sharp knife or saw after the turning and finishing is done. At the headstock end it will be necessary to cut a 'pin', or round tenon, to fit into the base. This is done with a sharp parting tool, using a woodworker's vernier caliper.

Vernier caliper in use measuring the pin on the base of a table lamp, so that projecting pins can be used to mark the base. This system ensures a good fit.

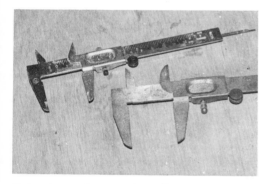

Columbus pattern vernier calipers.

These are very cheap, when compared with the cost of the real thing as used by engineers, and they are a most useful item, since they are ideal for this common job of fitting round tenons into recesses or holes. The photograph gives a good idea of the appearance of the tool, and in this case the approach is to measure the diameter of the inside of the recess on the base, or rather to set the points of the caliper to it so that the other pairs of jaws

can be used to check the accuracy of the pin, which should be a push fit in the base. When this is done the shaping at the tailstock end can be completed, cutting in carefully until the workpiece trembles slightly, then removing the job from the lathe and finishing it off by hand.

An ordinary white PVA woodworking glue could be used for this project, but I have formed the habit of using either Cascamite or Aerolite, particularly for built-up woodturning blanks. The bottom of the base can if desired be covered with self-adhesive green baize, which can be purchased from most large DIY establishments. If this is used it should be cut to a circle a little larger than the base, and carefully trimmed after it has been applied. This can be done with a really sharp craft knife or a razor-blade, being careful not to harm the wood.

7 Vases, Egg Cups and Goblets

By this time the beginner should be gaining some confidence, though this is best acquired slowly, too much being as bad as too little in the early days. The items discussed in this section are popular lines which always sell well if nicely turned.

A small vase is an interesting project to take us further into chuck work, and items like goblets and egg cups have their own particular problems. An egg cup is an ideal item for a beginner's first attempt at objects which are hollowed and have a stem. Once these can be made with ease, the more difficult aspects such as the making of wine glasses and goblets, which are taller and have thin stems, will not be quite so daunting.

VASES

A block of 3-inch-square hardwood, 5 or 6 inches long, will do very well for a vase, and some turners like to drill these out with a 1-inch or 1½-inch drill to a little short of the desired depth before mounting the blank on the lathe. This is not essential, but it does make the job a little easier. The ends of the blank should have been cut dead square; if not, they should be trimmed before the job is mounted. The larger woodscrew chuck can be used, and I often use only the centre screw.

Extra screws do help, but their length should be such that they do not penetrate the wood more than about ½ inch, or they may be uncovered as the foot is shaped. Always pre-drill for the screws of these chucks, using a drill bit of the correct size.

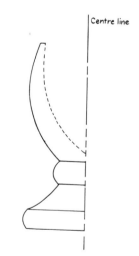

Suggested shape for small flower vase.

Once the job has been firmly mounted, a saw-toothed bit can be used in a Jacobs pattern chuck in the tailstock to open up the blank. Ideally the lathe should run as slowly as possible for these cutters, but no lathe I have seen will run much below 400

66

Saw-toothed bit: expensive but very efficient.

it is freshly ground and used carefully. Scrapers are never as efficient as chisels and gouges, but they have to be employed wherever it is impossible to work with the bevels of chisels or gouges rubbing the work, and they are at their best when cutting end grain, as is the case here. Heavy cuts must not be taken, or the wood will be badly torn, and the tool may suddenly grab and so loosen the wood on the chuck. Remember that scrapers must always be kept flat on the toolrest, and must never be pointed upwards. Since the bevel of a scraper is not involved, only the edge contacting the wood, it does not matter whether the cuts are taken from the outside into the hole, or from the bottom of the hole outwards. One new problem arises as the work proceeds, however, in that the waste cannot get away, so the job has to be stopped from time to time so that the shavings can be raked out and progress inspected. Make sure that the bottom of the hollow is as smooth as possible, and that there is neither a pimple nor a small depression there. One or other is quite likely, and can be very annoying if discovered after all else has gone well.

When the inside is satisfactory, the toolrest can be positioned along the work in readiness for the final shaping, and at this point the beginner can decide whether or not to use a plug. The inside of the job should be thoroughly sanded before proceeding, using sanding sealer as required, and some workers like to fit a small tapered wooden plug into the end of the job, so that the tailstock can be brought up to provide extra support. Ideas like this are all very well, but they frequently bring problems of their own, and there are two such inherent here. First, unless the lathe centres are exactly in line the use of such a plug may push the wood slightly off-

rpm, which is still too fast. The problem is that although this type of cutter is very efficient, it is also extremely expensive, and will become very hot unless great care is taken. The drilling should not be rushed, the drill being fed into the wood a little at a time, then withdrawn and allowed to cool. It is all too easy to turn these drills purple if the job is rushed, thereby ruining the temper of the steel. In order to ensure accuracy in the depth of the hole, it will be found helpful to wrap a strip of adhesive tape around the shank of the cutter to act as a guide.

When the drilling has been satisfactorily completed, the tailstock can be taken back to the other end of the lathe, and the drill and chuck removed. Nothing sharp should ever be left in a chuck in the tailstock, or the turner will one day suffer an injured elbow. Now, with the lathe running at whatever speed suits the operator, and the toolrest positioned across the end of the wood, the hollowing can be completed. A sharp parting tool can be used to remove some of the initial waste, but a small round-nosed scraper will be fine if centre; and second, very little tailstock pressure can be used on the plug, or the wood may split as it is turned thinner. I prefer to avoid 'crutches' of this kind if I can. If a simple shape is made, the roughing gouge can do most of the work, the final finish being achieved with a sharp spindle gouge and any detail put in with the point of a skew chisel. The rule is 'work slowly', rushing jobs of this kind almost always leads to failure.

The inside of a vase of this type can be shaped to accept a small glass tumbler from the local supermarket, or the vase can be finished inside and out with one of the two-part catalyst resins, which are totally waterproof. It is as well to do as little abrasive work as possible on wood where the grain is running lengthwise, as here, in fact I normally do none at all, but if it is felt necessary only fine-grade abrasive should be used. The inside is a different story, of course, since a scraper has been used, and a thorough sanding must always follow a scraper.

EGG CUPS AND GOBLETS

For reasons which have always eluded me, the humble egg cup is one of the most popular items made on the woodturner's lathe, and one of the most readily saleable. It is also a very nice little project for the beginner who has some practice behind him or her. A fact which escapes the observation of many people, however, is that this is one of the best ways into the difficult art of copy turning, about which more later. Egg cups are usually sold in sets, and frequently these are on trays or stands, so the egg cups should be as nearly identical as is reasonably possible. One can cheat a little, in that if one shape is

adopted, and fifty or sixty are made, it is quite easy to pick out good sets of four or six from the bulk stock, adding new ones as they come off the lathe. In this case, however, the production of that quantity might take some time, so why not make just one set, as a test of progress?

The first move will be to cut some small blocks of hardwood – beech would be excellent – or the more open-grained oak. The blocks should be about 2 inches square, a fraction over if possible, and $2\frac{1}{2}$ inches long. The smaller of the woodscrew chucks is used, to allow tool access to the base of the cup, and the block should, as always, be pre-drilled for the screw. Have the block screwed on as tightly as possible, but don't overdo this and strip the thread of the screw in the wood. It should also be noted that there is only one screw in use, and this is going into end grain, which is not the best place for screws. Blunt tools and bad techniques will have the job off the chuck in no time.

The best way to go about this sort of work is to make one egg cup and use it as a master for the rest. Run the block down almost, but not quite, to a cylinder, using the roughing gouge in the normal manner,

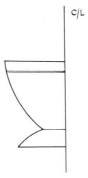

A simple shape for a beginner's first attempt at an egg cup.

taking light cuts. The end of the work is then trimmed across with a parting tool, removing very little wood but making the face of the job very slightly concave. This is to ensure peripheral contact on the chuck when it is removed and reversed, and to enable it to stand on a flat surface without wobbling. Drill a hole at the centre to accept the chuck screw, and reverse the work on the chuck.

The next operation must be the hollowing of the cup, which has to be done before the blank is weakened by shaping the stem. The toolrest is set up across the face of the job. It may be that the blank is now slightly off-centre, but as it was not run right down to the required diameter in the first process, there is no problem. The hollowing can be done in amateur fashion, by the laborious method of scraping, but the professional way of removing most of the waste very quickly is to use a sharp $\frac{1}{4}$-inch spindle gouge, the bevel of which should be fairly steep. This tool removes wood very quickly, but it is usually necessary to finish the job with a sharp scraper because the operation of the gouge becomes more difficult as the hollowing proceeds. There is a certain knack in the use of the small spindle gouge for this purpose, which will never be forgotten once it has been acquired. Some people pick this up rapidly, while others seem to have trouble. The thing is to check carefully on what is being done with the tool, and to persevere.

The toolrest should be slightly below the centre of the wood, and I always start cutting at the outer edge, swinging the cut through to the centre. If the cutting is begun at the centre, working out towards the edge cut by cut, there is likely to be constant trouble with the gouge skidding at the start of the cut, because, as is the case when cutting concave curves between centres, there is nothing to support the bevel until the cut has travelled a little way into the wood. The gouge is used as spindle gouges normally are, in a position where it is half on its back and half on its side, the cutting being done with the section of the edge which lies between the centre of the edge and the corner. The action is a scooping one: the handle of the tool *must* swing as the cut proceeds, to shape the curve and to keep the bevel in correct contact. If enough practice has been done on concave curves between centres, there should not be much trouble with this one. On no account must the gouge be allowed to pass the central point of the wood at the end of the cut, or it will contact the 'upstream' side of the job which will lift it and slam it back on to the toolrest.

This cutting should continue until it seems to be becoming a little awkward, at which point a really sharp round-nosed scraper takes over to finish the operation. If the scraper really is sharp it will remove streamers of fine shavings. If it is merely producing little heaps of dust which have to be shaken off occasionally, it is blunt. If the thumb is placed on top of the scraper blade above the contact point with the toolrest, the scraper can be pivoted as it moves along, facilitating the production of a smooth and continuous curve. Some turners like to drill a small hole in the end of the block before starting the hollowing, to a set depth, so that the hole acts as a depth gauge.

When the hollowing is completed, the interior of the cup should be inspected carefully to make quite sure that the dreaded pimple is not present at the centre, and that there are no nasty ridges anywhere. If there is a pimple, it can be removed by placing the edge of the scraper just below the offending phenomenon and lowering the handle. The lathe, of course, is running during this job.

When the interior is quite satisfactory, it must be sanded and, if necessary, treated with sanding sealer and sanded again. This should not be left until the whole job is finished, especially if the stem of the egg cup is to be thin, as the strain on the stem during the sanding may be too much. Accidents of this kind always happen to the best piece of work the workshop has seen in years.

The toolrest can now be repositioned for the shaping of the outside of the job, and the wood can be taken down to its required maximum diameter by means of the roughing gouge. This operation should remove any off-centring caused when the block was reversed. It helps to mark carefully the points at which the foot meets the stem, and where the stem meets the base of the cup, these being the two most important references, but do not make the common mistake of removing the wood down to the required maximum diameter of the stem by means of a succes-

sion of parting-tool cuts, in the hope that this will facilitate the shaping of the cup and the stem. This weakens the job too much, and when the cup is shaped there may be a most annoying twitch in the job which throws up ripples on the surface as the curve is cut. Once these appear they are not easy to remove. One answer would be to take the soft option and make egg cups which either have thick stems or no stems at all. The old saying 'nothing ventured, nothing gained' is still true, and what is meant to be gained here is experience.

The best method here, for a novice, is to make one or two parting-tool cuts at the point where the junction of stem and cup has been marked, removing sufficient wood to permit the start of the shaping of the cup, trying to finish the cup section while there is plenty of wood to support it. A little experimenting with this will soon provide proficiency, and most turners will work out little methods of their own. The shape I have shown is a favourite of mine which I use as a practice piece for students, and it can look very good when turned well.

8 Bowl-turning

Since this book is intended as a beginner's guide, emphasis has been placed on spindle-turning, in which a complete novice has the best chance of learning to use the tools with the minimum of danger. Incidents such as skidding of tools, or minor digs, are quite naturally demoralising, but digs which occur in bowl-turning are very much more so due to the relatively large mass of the material. There is also a need to work with considerable projection of the gouge over the edge of the toolrest when hollowing bowls, so that the tool is far less easy to control if the operator is unskilled. In view of all this, I advise my students to leave the turning of bowls until they have become competent in spindle work, by which time correct tool manipulation will come naturally to them.

The subject of bowl-turning, if thoroughly covered, could fill a complete book, but here I have explained the basics, giving sufficient guidance for newcomers to the craft who want to try some small bowls. Before thrusting the trusty $\frac{3}{8}$-inch deep-fluted gouge into an expensive bowl blank which is whirling away on the lathe, however, it would be as well to give a little thought to what is involved in the process, and the first significant point is that bowls are almost exclusively made from discs of wood. A vast number of other projects will be made from discs, not just bowls, so the fundamentals of the matter must be made clear.

For the purposes of this book a 'stick' is a turning blank in which the grain runs roughly parallel to the lathe bed, and a 'disc' is a circular blank cut from a board, so that the grain runs across the disc. Sticks are rather easier for beginners to cope with, and there are one or two points about discs which need to be clarified. Since a disc is cut from a board it has end grain, where the ends of the fibres are exposed, and face grain, where the length of the fibres can be found. It is not so much the end grain which causes finishing problems as what is known as the 'quarter grain', this being the areas lying between the end and face grain parts. In these areas the gouge, particularly if it is not really sharp, will tend to lift the ends of the fibres, creating rough patches, and these can be most annoying. The phenomenon will vary in severity with different timbers, but there are ways and means of coping with it.

At this point it is necessary to point out a potential danger, which exists mainly with fairly thin discs such as may be used in turning bases for table lamps, ash trays, butter dishes, wooden plates and similar projects. In this sort of work, the turner should not stand in line with the disc when cutting its edges, nor should spectators be permitted to do so, because a dig-in can easily split a section of wood from the disc and hurl it quite violently from the lathe. This section will have sharp ends, and eyes have been lost in this way. The answer is firstly not to dig in, and secondly to make sure that the flight path is clear. If in doubt, wear one of the light-weight visors which are readily available from suppliers of woodturning equipment.

It is commonly believed that expert woodturners always use 'long and strong' tools. In my experience this is not true, and most of the people whom I would re-gard as true experts use them rarely, and only for the purpose for which they are intended. This is in the shaping of objects which call for an unusual amount of pro-jection of the tool over the edge of the toolrest, as was common years ago in the turning of huge newel posts for staircases, billiard-table legs of enormous girth, and so on. In fact, these tools are extremely expensive, awkward and cumbersome in use, giving little 'feel' of the cut, and they are by no means as easy to sharpen as the standard tools. Sharpening a 'long and strong' tool also takes much longer, since the area of the bevel is much greater. I use them when I have to, but not otherwise. The whole point here, of course, is that standard tools, if projected too far off the toolrest, will begin to 'flutter', which spoils the cut and can lead to a dig-in. A dig with a standard tool projected well for-ward of the toolrest could break the blade, and the broken section flying off could cause serious injury.

The $\frac{3}{8}$-inch deep-fluted gouge is the tool for bowls, though bigger versions are used on the larger bowl projects, but it is only on these very large bowls that I use a 'long and strong'. The standard is far more pleasant to handle.

If you want to learn to ride a horse, it is sensible to begin with a nice docile beast, placid and even-tempered. So it should be with bowl-turning. There is no point in hanging a great lump of wood, 18 inches in diameter and 4 inches thick, on the lathe and attacking it with a gouge, in fact the odds are that this sort of approach would put a beginner off bowls for life. An even-grained piece of timber, without knots, for the first few bowls anyway, will do well, and beech or sycamore would be good choices. Those who can restrain their impatience will do well to start their bowl-turning careers by shaping small discs of softwood, any pine of reasonable quality will do, using blanks about 6 inches in diameter by 2 inches thick. A few sessions should be devoted to learning how to shape the outside of a bowl, vary-ing the shapes made, the remains being consigned to the scrap bin when they have become too small. This can be followed by periods of experimenting with the hol-lowing of bowls, again using the eventual remains as firewood; then some attempts can be made at completed bowls from this sort of blank. It will immediately be apparent that turning bowls from pine is not easy, though it can be done, and they look very nice indeed. The problem with a material like this will be in getting a smooth finish, but I will explain the secrets of this later.

There are differences between the turn-ing of bowls and the production of spindles which may cause problems in the early stages of learning the craft, but in some ways bowl-turning is depressingly easy, which may account for the fact that there are many people who turn very little else. My point is that the shaping of a correctly proportioned concave curve, or a convex shape, between centres, will call for the turning of both the left- and the right-hand sections of the shape, and the blending of them without leaving any roughness. In bowl work this is not the case, as a little thought will reveal. A smooth cut from the edge to the centre deals with the whole area, there is no question of having to cut the left- and right-hand sides of a bowl separately, so that whether or not the shape produced is appealing, it will certainly be balanced. This fact, together with the very impressive shavings which stream from a gouge as it cuts sweetly inside a bowl, seems to delight some turners, but bowls are only a tiny part of the craft, and those who really want to call themselves experts will need to work long and hard until they are good at copy work, which is the backbone of the trade.

Some of the older books on woodturning suggest that bowl blanks should be mounted on a faceplate for the turning of the outside of the bowl, and that the work should then be reversed on the faceplate for hollowing. I have never understood the reasoning here. There seems to be no advantage in this system, and there is an inherent snag, in that work reversed in this manner has a nasty habit of ending up just a fraction off-centre, so that the walls of the finished bowl vary in thickness. If the faceplate used is not too large for the size of blank, it is quite easy to turn the bowl in one mounting, and indeed this is preferable. Whether the outside is turned before the hollowing of the inside, or vice versa, seems to me to be a matter of individual preference since I have used both approaches with equal success.

The size of the faceplate should be considered since, as I remarked earlier, most lathes fail to offer a small faceplate, which is a most useful item. The version supplied by the makers of the Avon lathe, is a real blessing for many projects. It is fairly obvious that if the faceplate is too large it will obstruct the free passage of the gouge when the outside shaping is done, and the only satisfactory way round this is to interpose a disc of scrap softwood between the faceplate and the job, which is time-consuming. If no small faceplate (4- or 5-inch diameter) is available, the best answer is the larger of the woodscrew chucks, using additional screws in the holes provided. This chuck works well on small bowls, up to 8 or 9 inches in diameter, but a 5-inch steel faceplate is far better.

The use of faceplates or screw chucks in bowl work, and in the turning of other disc-based projects, gives a stronger and more reliable mounting than would be the case if goblets or vases were being made, since in the case of discs the screws are into face grain, rather than end grain. The holding power of a screw in the end grain of timber is not good by any standards, but if short No. 14 screws are used they will give a very good grip indeed on discs. Those fortunate enough to have an expanding collet chuck may like to use it for bowl work, but care must be taken to see that it is fitted correctly to the bowl blank, and that it is tightened securely. Provided that such care is taken, there should be no trouble as these chucks give a far more secure mounting than their appearance suggests.

It might be expected that as I am now discussing the use of a different gouge from those so far covered, there will be differences in technique, but fundamentally the use of the $\frac{3}{8}$-inch deep-fluted gouge is the same as that of a gouge of any other pattern, inasmuch as the same three rules must be obeyed. The area of the bevel which immediately surrounds the part of

Roughing out the shape of a small bowl. Cuts must run downhill.

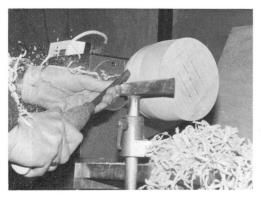

The tool moves from right to left in cutting the base section.

the edge which is cutting must rub the wood. All cuts are made downhill, rather than uphill. The part of the edge which is used must be *directly* supported by the toolrest. If these rules are followed faithfully, there will be few problems, and it will also be found that the tool movements learned in working between centres are significant. The fact is that the tool movement in hollowing the curved interior of

a bowl is the same as that used when making concave shapes on a spindle, and the tool manipulation in shaping the outside of a curved bowl does not differ from that employed in making convex curves on other projects. This means that those who have practised for some time on spindle-turning will already know a good deal of what they need for the making of bowls.

Lathes vary in the facilities they provide for bowl and other forms of disc-turning.

Keep the toolrest close to the work to avoid snatching and possible tearing of the surface.

Some make no special provision, merely giving a fairly large distance between the headstock spindle and the bed, and users of such machines generally work happily enough within the limits of the lathe. Other machines have spindles which pass right through the headstock, so providing a facility for mounting disc work on the outboard end, where special provision is made for the fitting of a toolrest holder. A third system, as shown in the illustrations of the Avon lathe, is more complex, but very efficient and useful. This system per-

The swivelling headstock facility of the Avon lathe is used for large-diameter discs. Note the sturdy support for the toolrest holder.

mits the headstock to be rotated through 90 degrees, so that there is ample room for the turning of a large disc, a very solid adjustable bracket being provided to support the toolrest holder. A point worth noting about lathes which are designed for turning on the opposite end of the spindle, as in the second example, is that they are not a good choice for those who are short of working space. This system forces the turner to stand facing the end of the machine, which means that a reasonable area of floor must be kept clear for this purpose.

When turning bowls up to about 8 inches in diameter, I tend to keep the lathe up near its top speed, which is likely to be a little over 2000 rpm, dropping the speed as required on larger diameters. Here again, the beginner should select a speed which seems comfortable and reasonable, and things will be helped a lot in the learning stage by having the bowl turning blanks cut accurately to a circle, and centred with accuracy so that vibration is kept to a minimum.

The turning of very large bowls or other disc projects is usually outside the scope of lathes sold for the hobbyist, because even if very large diameters can be swung, there is no provision for the low speed which such work requires. Those who become 'hooked' on the turning of bowls may elect eventually to purchase what is known as a 'bowl-turning head'. This is not a lathe in the ordinary sense, but is merely a spindle mounted on a pedestal. The spindle is double-ended, like that of a grinder, with provision for the fitting of faceplates at either end and with toolrests which can be adjusted in the same way as those on a normal lathe. These machines are designed purely for the turning of bowls and large discs, and the speed-range covers the requirements of such work.

It is advisable, though not essential, to have timber which is to be used for bowl-turning planed on one face, then run through a thicknesser to level the other face and bring it parallel to the first. If this is not possible, one face should be planed flat before fitting the blank to the faceplate, which will ensure that the mounting is as firm as possible.

The following description of the turning of a bowl is not as detailed as when I am instructing in my workshop, but it gives as much guidance as possible within the space limitations of a book and should prove helpful to those attempting their first bowl. The $\frac{3}{8}$-inch deep-fluted gouge will be used, and should be carefully ground before starting the job. Note also that bowl work, particularly with some timbers, is rough on tool edges which require frequent trips to the grinder. Since the sharpening of a gouge on a grinder takes about twenty seconds, however, this is not really a problem. I am describing the full process here, but normally when bowl-turning I like to leave the job at a stage just short of completion for about twenty-four hours to allow for any movement caused by relief of stresses in the timber. If this is done, the final cuts will true up the bowl, and there should be no further trouble.

Beginners will find that if their first few bowls are turned from timber which is not quite bone dry, the work will be easier. Very dry wood, particularly elm, is difficult and unpleasant to turn.

This first bowl will be turned with the gouge referred to above, and a round-nosed scraper. The sharpening of scrapers seems to cause considerable misunderstanding among novices, so a short discussion will not be out of place.

It is certainly not a good idea to have too many scrapers, but it is advisable to use standard ones for hollowing in chuck operations such as the making of vases, goblets, egg cups and so on. Those used in bowl work should be of heavier section, since they will work with greater projection from the edge of the toolrest, and heavy-duty bowl-turning scrapers can be obtained quite easily. The blades of these heavy scrapers will not flex in use, which could cause serious trouble. There are only four points of which a beginner needs to be aware when first using scrapers, and very little actual skill is called for. Note that scrapers must be kept flat on the toolrest, neither side being lifted clear, at least until a fair amount of practice-time has passed. They must *never* be pointed upwards inside a bowl; this can lead to a serious accident, so keep the scraper horizontal, or better still pointing slightly downward. The third point is that they must never be pushed hard into the wood, or they will tear it badly. It is better to take several light cuts with one of these tools than one heavy one.

The fourth point concerns the sharpen-

Partly turned yew bowl. This colourful, dense timber turns well and responds quite well to a sharp scraper.

ing, which is quite unlike the procedure adopted when grinding gouges and chisels. The only occasion on which I will use the side of the grinding wheel, as distinct from the curved face of the stone, is immediately before grinding a scraper. The grinding is *not* done on the side of the wheel, but a new cutting 'burr' cannot be put on top of the remains of an old one, so I place the flat upper surface of the tool against the side of the wheel for a second or so to remove the remains of the previous burr, then grind the tool with its bevel flat on the curved face of the wheel, swinging it round once only, with sparks showing at the edge. This produces a good working bevel for general use. Some people grind scrapers with the blade inverted, the tool being upside down, which is said to produce a better burr. What it in fact produces is a more pronounced burr,

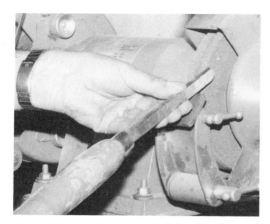

The old 'burr' of a scraper is 'wiped off' on the side of the wheel before regrinding.

which will cut well but is fragile and quickly destroyed by the wood. A third approach is to grind the bevel, remove the resulting burr from the tool by means of an oilstone, and 'ticket' the edge as a cabinet-maker would do with his scraper. This process takes a while to learn, in that there is a knack to it, and it produces an even more fragile cutting edge. I am not recommending the ticketing of scrapers, but the process consists of turning up the extreme edge of the tool by pressure from a very hard steel rod, which is run quickly along it.

TURNING THE BOWL

Turning the Outside

There are numerous approaches to the turning of bowls, but here I will use one which I have not so far mentioned, which is to turn the outside with the blank mounted on a faceplate, then reverse the blank into a hollow wooden chuck. The circular blank is mounted securely on a faceplate, the turner sets the lathe at a speed which suits him or her, and the job can start. The toolrest must be positioned carefully if the face of the job is to be trued up, since it is necessary for the tool to be on the toolrest, the bevel rubbing correctly in the cut, and for the cut to run precisely to the centre of the blank. If the toolrest is too high, a properly executed cut will not run to the centre. A small uncut circular area will remain, and there is the danger that a beginner may try to reach this by lifting the handle of the gouge, whereupon a skid or even a dig-in is very likely. The best answer to this is to place the gouge on the toolrest, with its bevel rubbing, and with the lathe switched off. A 'dummy run' across the work will immediately show whether or not the toolrest height is accurate, and any adjustment can be made before starting the job.

If the wood was originally rough-sawn, or dirty, or both, the clean surface produced by the first cut can be examined for small cracks, and if any are present the blank should be rejected, since a beginner will not be able to judge the potential danger with accuracy. If all is well, the toolrest is positioned across the edge of the work, at a height which is comfortable for the worker and reasonably close to the work. A small gap is in order, but not one which has a magnitude of several inches. Here I am describing the bowl-turning procedure with the outside being shaped before the inside, because I intend reversing the blank into a wooden chuck for the hollowing. Normally there would be no particular significance in which part of the job was done first.

The movement of the gouge in the shaping of a curve or curves on the outside of a bowl is very similar to that employed when making curves between centres and, as with the spindle gouge, most of the cutting is done with the sections of the edge which lie between the centre and the corner. The corners themselves should not touch the wood, since they cannot cut and will make deep rings. We now find one difference, however, in that whereas the centre of the edge of a spindle gouge should not be used, the centre of this disc-turning gouge is frequently used in the early stages while bringing the blank to a perfectly true disc.

At the beginning of this book I mentioned that a dig-in while bowl-turning is a more spectacular and disturbing matter than a similar event between centres, due to the grain disposition of the blank, the mass of the wood, and at times the greater projection of the tool from the toolrest. This is quite true, but there is no reason to approach bowl-turning in fear and trepidation. The answer, of course, is not to dig in, and this merely requires some logical thought when presenting the gouge to the wood, as against a 'deep breath and here goes' approach. The gouge will dig if it is lifted clear of the toolrest while cutting, and this can be done by an inexperienced worker without conscious knowledge. It is also likely to dig if any attempt is made to cut without the support of the bevel. Occasionally some semi-skilled person wishing to demonstrate that a little learning is a dangerous thing will suggest in print that the bevels do not need to rub, but such nonsense can lead to injury, and should be disregarded. If the bevel is not rubbing, the tool is being offered to the wood with too great an angle of attack. This gives a scraping action, which quickly destroys the edge and can precipitate a nasty dig. If scraping is unavoidable, it *must* be done with scrapers, not with cutting tools.

Correct tool presentation is that which offers the maximum of safety with the maximum of efficiency, and anything which conforms to that definition is entirely in order. Such tool presentation becomes instinctive in time, but it is a source of frustration in the early stages. The problem can be greatly reduced, however, by thinking the matter out, and never attempting to cut unless satisfied that the approach is safe. This means placing the gouge on the toolrest with its handle *low* and positioning the *heel* of the bevel on the wood. It cannot dig in, in fact it can't even cut. The tool is now kept on the toolrest while the angle of attack is adjusted until, with pressure against the wood, a shaving of the desired thickness is produced. Try this with the lathe switched off, to get the slow motion effect, rotating the wood slowly by hand. It will be better not to start the turning of the bowl until this matter is quite clear.

It is vitally important for the handle of the gouge to be kept well down, so that the bevel rubs firmly upon the surface which is revealed by the removal of the shaving. In this condition, if the handle is lowered a fraction, the cut will cease, whereas if it is lifted *very* slightly and pressure against the wood is maintained, a deeper cut will result. Safe and effective control of the depth of cut is extremely important in bowl work, and will be obtainable only by the methods I have described.

Keeping all this well in mind, the outside of the disc can be brought to a smooth circle by means of a number of controlled cuts, whereupon the lathe should be stopped so that the surface can be examined. The end grain of a disc will always

The outside of a blank is trued up with a freshly ground $\frac{3}{8}$ inch deep-fluted gouge.

feel rougher than the face grain at this stage, but it should nevertheless have been cut cleanly. Two roughened areas may well be discovered in the quarter grain areas, but these can be corrected by suitable tool techniques during the ensuing shaping operation.

The movements required in putting a good convex shape on the outside of a bowl are much the same as in putting one

The final cuts on a bowl need careful bevel control and a freshly ground edge.

on work between centres. The job is started about a $\frac{1}{2}$-inch in from the front edge of the blank, cutting from left to right and swinging the handle round to form the curve. The work should not be hurried, and if the gouge is freshly ground, curly shavings will fly from the wood. The small curve produced by the first cut is enlarged by the subsequent cuts, starting a little nearer the back of the disc each time, pressing the gouge against the wood and controlling the depth of cut carefully by the swing of the handle. The aim should be for each cut to be continuous, rather than a series of stops and starts, and the swing of the handle is the key to this.

Since the intention with this particular bowl is to reverse it into a wooden chuck for the hollowing, a definite base has to be formed, the edges of which should be parallel to the lathe bed. In other words, there should be a base about $\frac{1}{4}$ inch thick, the sides of which are at 90 degrees to the bottom of the bowl. Some turners try to cut this base by means of a parting tool, but it is not easy to produce in this fashion and is better shaped by stopping the last one or two cuts of the curve shaping short of their true end, so leaving the 'step' required. A base of this kind looks quite attractive, but is also functional, since it is this base which is driven into the wooden chuck.

Most faceplate work, however well it has been cut, will require some abrasive paper because of the nature of the grain in the disc, and in this particular job this should be applied as soon as the outside has been shaped. Really coarse paper must not be used because it forms deep scratches in the wood which can be difficult to remove. Additionally, all cutting on any surface must be finished before abrasive paper is used or abrasive dust in the wood will take the edge straight off the tool. Sandpaper as such is not used in machine woodwork, the most common abrasive papers being garnet, which is orange in colour, or aluminium oxide, which is widely used for sander belts and comes in a range of colours. Abrasive papers are described by the size of the mesh through which the grains pass during manufacture, this being based on a square inch of mesh. A paper of 100 grit will have grains which have passed through a mesh having a hundred holes to the square inch. I would suggest 120 as a good grade for the initial sanding of a bowl, followed eventually by 240. I rarely sand work between centres, and if I do I restrict this to 320 followed by very fine steel wool. Note also that abrasive papers can be obtained as 'open coat' or 'closed coat', and the latter is not desirable for woodturning. Open-coat paper has the grains more widely spaced, and works quite well, but closed-coat will clog quickly when used on a lathe.

Preparing the Chuck

Once the outside of the bowl is judged to be satisfactory the blank can be removed from the faceplate and set aside while the wooden chuck is prepared. This is a simple operation, but it requires care since the chuck needs to be exact in its internal dimensions. The term 'chuck' is perhaps a trifle grandiose in this context, in view of the fact that the thing simply consists of a disc of wood in which a recess of suitable size has been cut with a parting tool, but it is a chuck for all that.

A disc an inch or so thick will do, and it can be of softwood or hardwood, but it must be sound and completely free of cracks. It is screwed on to the faceplate, and the toolrest is set up across its face. The base of the bowl blank is now accurately measured, and this measurement is transferred to the disc, the size of the required recess being indicated by a pencil line. It is best to make the recess a fraction on the small side at first, enlarging it carefully once it has been cut on a trial and error basis, until the base of the bowl can be tapped into the recess and is firmly held. If it should be a little slack, the inside of the recess can be soaked with water, which will swell the grain and improve the fit. Alternatively a piece of brown paper can be laid across the recess before the blank is fitted. The cuts made during the hollowing tend to push the blank into the chuck rather than pull it out, and I have made hundreds of bowls this way without trouble.

I am not suggesting that a beginner's very first bowl should be made in this way, but the system has advantages for those who have no expanding collet chuck, as it provides a method of hollowing a bowl without the need to worry about screws. If a faceplate is used for the whole job, the screws are a nuisance, and the bowl cannot be made as deep as is possible by the hollow chuck method. The screw holes left from the first mounting of the blank are, of course, removed by the hollowing.

Hollowing the Blank

From the letters and telephone calls I receive it appears that many novices are confused by the somewhat controversial issue of exactly where to start the hollowing. Should this, they ask, be at the outer edge, at the centre, or at some intermediate point? To a large extent this is academic, and the thing is to try all these approaches, selecting the one found preferable. There are some points worth considering, however. If the hollowing is started at the outer edge, leaving enough wood for the desired wall thickness, only the first cut is at risk in the sense of the gouge skidding. In this first cut the edge has to be placed on the wood, and has no support from the bevel until it has entered. All subsequent cuts can be commenced by placing the bevel inside the rim and adjusting the angle of attack to achieve the desired depth of cut. Note that here the shape is concave so, as was the case between centres, the handle of the gouge has to be swung backwards to keep the bevel rubbing. Some workers in fact like to have two $\frac{3}{8}$-inch deep-fluted gouges, one of which is ground with a *convex* bevel, and is used for hollowing bowls which have curved interiors.

An alternative, which is quite acceptable, is to start the hollowing at the centre of the blank, and this is the method I employ on all bowls under about 12 inches in

diameter. It requires a little more skill, but only in the presentation of the gouge at the start of the cut, which if not done correctly will cause a skid. This problem was also present in the making of a concave shape between centres, and the knack is soon acquired. Neither of these versions of the hollowing procedure is really satisfactory on a very large bowl, because there is a phenomenon which can cause frustration for inexperienced workers. This is soon discovered if a big bowl is hollowed from the centre, working outwards, or from the outside and cutting towards the centre. As the wall of the bowl becomes thinner it will flex under the pressure of the gouge, causing a rippling of the surface which is hard to eliminate. The problem can be overcome by starting the hollowing about a third of the way between the outside edge and the centre, and cutting alternately from either direction to form a V-shaped trench. This trench is enlarged until the wall of the bowl is down to finished thickness, and at this stage

Hollowing of smaller bowls starts at the centre, working back to the wall thickness.

Large bowls are hollowed as shown here, cutting alternately from each side of the 'trench'.

A large amount of wood remains at the centre when the interior of the bowl wall is nearly complete, preventing whipping of the wood under tool pressure.

A curved bowl-turning rest may be useful, but beware of 'bounce', which can cause tearing of the wood, or even a dig-in.

there is still a fair amount of wood to be removed from the central area. This is cut away last, when it has served its purpose of acting like a web in a casting to give strength to the bowl wall.

The wood left at the centre can be removed by a series of cuts, and any small mound left at the centre can be smoothed away with the gouge, working towards the centre. The photographs will help to clarify this. At about this stage a scraper may be needed to finish the interior. Whether or not the job can be completed with a gouge will depend upon the shape, which may prevent the bevel from being kept in contact. It will also depend upon the ability of the turner, who may well find the gouge more awkward to control as the bowl becomes deeper. It is possible to purchase curved toolrests for working inside bowls, and I have shown one here, but I must say that I dislike the idea. The real trouble with it is that it looks like an excellent device to those who have never used it, but it has a weakness, in both

senses of the word. The object of a curved bowl-turning rest is to reduce the overhang of the tool when working inside the bowl, but at the deepest part of the bowl the gouge or scraper is supported by the section of the toolrest which is furthest from its supporting pin. This gives rise to flexing in the toolrest, which can in turn lead to digging in. If one of these rests is used, the cutting should be shallow and carefully done.

It is frequently necessary to use a scraper inside a bowl if a point is reached where the bevel of the gouge can no longer be used to support the cutting edge. A little thought will show that a bowl which curves in at the top is an example of this. The scraper overcomes this problem, but will not produce as good a finish as the gouge, and on most timbers two rough patches will appear where the scraper has crossed the grain. This can be removed by abrasive work, with the aid of a little sanding sealer, but bowls should be made without the use of a scraper if possible.

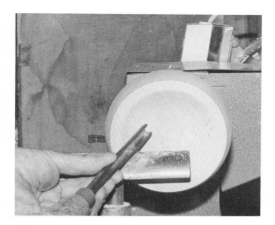

A bowl of these proportions can be completed without resorting to scrapers, and little abrasive work will be called for.

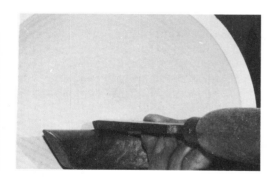

A heavy scraper may be useful in some bowls, but must not be pointed upwards.

When such a tool is used it must be as sharp as possible, which means that it needs to be taken to the grinder frequently, and it must not be pushed hard into the wood or it will badly tear the surface.

Sanding Bowls

At the end of this book I have dealt with finishes used in woodturning, and finishing techniques, in as much detail as space would permit, but a few reflections on the sanding of bowls may help here. It is often easier to bring the outside of a bowl to a really fine finish with abrasives than it is the inside, but many turners now sand the insides of bowls by means of a pad sander attached to an electric drill. A pad sander is a small flat circular disc of a spongy material, to which discs of abrasive material are attached, usually by means of Velcro. The drill is switched on, and the pad is applied to the downward side of the bowl interior while the lathe is running. This may sound dangerous, but it is quite safe, and is common practice. The disc is applied so that an area near its lower edge contacts the bowl, and the system is remarkably efficient.

Another aspect of abrasive work in disc-turning is worthy of mention, this being the use of reversing switches on

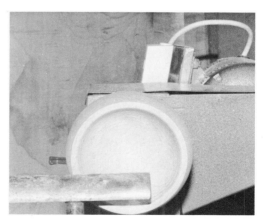

The bowl ready for sanding sealer and finishing procedures.

lathes to permit the work to be rotated in the reverse direction for sanding. Just as running a comb through hair persuades the fibres to lie in one direction, so the grains of abrasive paper produce a situation in which the fibres of the wood which are causing the roughness all lie with their ends facing into the direction of rotation. This reduces the efficiency of the abrasive paper, and reversing the direction of rotation is quite effective. Unfortunately the makers of lathes do not make provision for their equipment to be run backwards, and items such as chucks and faceplates, which are normally self-locking in use, become self-unlocking, sometimes with disastrous results. Unless some positive arrangement is made to prevent chucks and faceplates from unscrewing themselves, this system should be avoided. I am aware that one sometimes reads magazine articles in which this sort of thing is recommended, but not all magazine articles are to be trusted. Safety should be the first consideration, so *please* don't take chances of this nature.

When a bowl is finished, and ready for abrasive work, it should be given a good soaking with a sanding sealer. This is a liquid with rapid drying properties. It will raise the grain of the wood just as water would do, but will then set hard and lock the raised grain in position for sanding. If a sanding sealer is not used, the surface will be unsealed, and the end grain of the bowl will soak up polish more freely than the face grain, so that the bowl ends up with shiny areas and darkened rough areas. The two main types of sanding sealer are either shellac based or are mainly clear cellulose. The latter sometimes has a quantity of French chalk mixed with it to give it 'body'. If this is the case the sealer should be shaken vigorously before use on light-coloured timbers, and not shaken when used on dark ones. The chalk precipitates out of the mixture, and is best left at the bottom of the tin when turning walnut or other dark woods as it can give an unpleasant grey cast to the finished job. Sanding sealer is also effective as a finish on work between centres, successive coats being cut back with fine steel wool and burnished with a soft cloth.

TIMBER FOR BOWLS

A final point in relation to bowl work – though if space permitted I could continue for quite a while – is that bowls can be turned from timber which is literally green, having only recently been cut.

The rough turning of really wet bowl blanks is quite straightforward, but extremely messy. Centrifugal force drives the moisture out, and it gets all over the place, but if the turner is not deterred by this the job is pleasant, in that wet timber turns far more easily than dry stuff. The procedure is to select a number of bowl blanks to be dealt with as a batch, and

Completed sycamore bowl, finished with sanding sealer only.

these will receive attention on a number of occasions until they are finally completed. The initial approach is to mount each one on the lathe, and with the $\frac{3}{8}$-inch deep-fluted gouge roughly shape the outside and remove about a quarter of the material from the inside. When each blank has been treated in this way they can all be hung up in an airy place in some old netting for a few weeks, out of direct sunlight. This is repeated with drying intervals until the bowls are done, and perfectly good results can be obtained. The point, of course, is that green timber is a great deal less expensive than seasoned stuff, so the idea has its attractions. A point to note is that if circular blanks are cut from really green wood for this purpose, they should be kept covered with damp shavings until the time comes to turn them, or they are likely to split badly on the end grain.

Elm is very popular with keen bowl-turners. Not the easiest of woods to turn, nevertheless it does look beautiful if well turned and polished. Pieces which have wild curly grain, or knots, should not be despised, since these often give the most striking results. Open knots in elm can be filled with brown sealing wax, as used in post offices, this being melted in with a match then filed smooth before final sanding.

9 Some Spindle Projects

LAMPS

Lamps of various kinds are very popular with amateur turners and represent a sensible project in the early days, there being nothing really difficult in their construction. However, once the first projects are undertaken where no drawing or pattern is used, and the project is the product of the turner's imagination, the question of proportion arises. Both table and standard lamps must have stability, so that they can take small knocks without immediately toppling over, which means that the width of the base must be in proportion to the stem, bearing in mind that the finished lamp will have a bulb holder and shade, which add weight at the top. There are no hard-and-fast rules about this, the matter is really one of common sense. It is also necessary when designing a lamp to visualise it complete with its shade. If this is overlooked, the lamp may seem fine when completed but look somehow wrong when the shade is fitted.

There is no need to purchase an expensive piece of timber for the job, in fact cheap material should be used for the first few attempts, and I have made many attractive lamps from pieces of pine. These can be painted or stained, or they can be left in their natural condition and polished. Natural pine artefacts are readily

saleable, since the demanding nature of pine as a turning material means that there is little well-turned stuff in the shops, and there are many people with pine furniture who are constantly looking for accessories to match it. Very pretty 'nursery lamps' can be made in pine and subsequently painted in bright colours, these being decorated with transfers of a suitable nature which can be bought from DIY or wallpaper shops.

Table lamps which are not too tall can often be made from one piece of wood, if it is sufficiently thick, but the majority of

A table lamp in beech: less than ten minutes' work for an experienced turner.

86

lamps consist of a stem and a base, which are separate turnings. In such cases a pin will be turned on the bottom of the stem, to fit into a hole which is drilled into the base or cut by means of a parting tool. Once the flex has been threaded through, the two parts can be firmly assembled with a good-quality adhesive such as Cascamite. The turning itself does not call for much in the way of description, since the shaping will be done by means of the cutting techniques already described. Remember that the $\frac{3}{8}$-inch deep-fluted gouge is a disc-turning gouge, so this is the tool to use, possibly in conjunction with a scraper, when making the base.

Standard lamps cannot usually have their stems turned in one length because they are too long for the vast majority of lathes, and in any event the turning of very long workpieces is not a task for a beginner. These lamps will have the stem turned in two sections, these being joined by means of a pin on the end of one, fitting tightly into a hole which is drilled into the other. The drilling of this hole should be done before the turning, and if the resulting hole is too large for the tailstock centre, a small wooden plug can be inserted.

The base of a standard lamp must be wide enough to give adequate support, and is usually made from quite thick timber to give weight. If the weight of the base is not considered to be sufficient, extra weight is sometimes added by inserting plugs of lead into the underside. This is not normally necessary, but may be a useful idea on some occasions. Some standard lamps have small turned feet fitted, but this is not particularly important. One point, however, is that a base with three such feet will stand firmly on most floors, which was of course the idea be-

hind the three-legged milking stool. A four-legged stool would not have been practical on cobbled or rough flagged floors.

There are kits available for most lathes to permit the turning of long holes, which is most frequently called for in lamp turning, and these work very well although the idea is rather primitive. Some beginners seem to be rather nervous when first faced with the problem of drilling through a long piece of timber, but the process is very simple and there is no need for concern. The facilities provided, or offered as optional extras, by various manufacturers do vary a little, but the principle remains essentially the same. Some lathes, like the Lazari Mini-Max, and the Tyme Avon and the smaller Cub, have tubular tailstock spindles through which the long auger can be passed. It is necessary to purchase a special tailstock centre which has a hole through its length. Lathes which do not have the facility for drilling through the tailstock usually offer a small drilling jig which fits into the toolrest holder and replaces the tailstock during drilling operations. Both systems work well once a little practice has been carried out with scrap wood.

The auger used is known as a 'shell auger', and the size normally used for lamps is $\frac{5}{16}$ inch, this producing a hole of the correct size to accept a metal-worker's $\frac{3}{8}$-inch Whitworth 'tap'. The tap cuts an internal thread to accept the thread of the brass 'nipple' which connects the bulb holder to the lamp. It is simple to operate the tap, and this process makes a good job of it, but the nipple can be pushed or knocked into the hole and held with a strong adhesive if preferred.

The question of whether the hole in a lamp should be drilled before or after the turning seems to be one of the eternal chestnuts which concern those with nothing better to do than start arguments through the woodworking magazines. Long-winded and specious argument is hardly likely to assist the progress of a beginner, or to increase the income of a professional, so I will simply point out here that either approach can be adopted, and I sometimes drill a lamp after it has been turned. It seems that most turners do drill the square blank beforehand, however, and there are several good reasons why. If the turning has gone well, and the subsequent drilling goes wrong for some reason, there is likely to be annoyance and frustration. If the lamp has been turned and polished, the finish may be spoiled during the drilling process, either by the handling of the lamp or by its being dropped and perhaps striking a sharp part of the lathe, so producing a dent. It is a choice for the individual, and I will leave it there.

Those who are truly experts in the sharpening of cutters in general may like to sharpen the auger very gently on rare occasions. Others would be well advised not to sharpen it, since their attentions may change the shape of the auger, which then may not run true. It should also be observed that there is a very tiny lip on the auger, which does the actual cutting, and if this is removed by constant sharpening the tool is useless.

A shell auger must not be fed into the rotating wood further than the length of its fluted section at one pass, or there will be no means of escape for the waste particles, the tool will jam and be overheated, and the job may be spoiled. It is taken in to the depth of the flute, then withdrawn, and the waste shaken from it. This process is repeated as many times as necessary. If the project is a short table lamp it is possible to drill almost all the way through, then remove the work from the lathe and finish the last little bit by hand. Longer lamps, however, need to be reversed in the lathe after a hole has been drilled to a little more than halfway along the length. When the material is reversed in this process, a special drive centre is used, which has a $\frac{5}{16}$-inch diameter pin protruding from it. This pin fits into the hole created by the initial drilling, so ensuring that the job is correctly centred. Once the wood has been reversed, and firmly mounted in the lathe, the drilling process is repeated and the two holes will meet. If there is any slight discrepancy in the alignment, this will be hidden away from sight, and so is unimportant.

The lamp base will be a straightforward piece of disc-turning, and a small faceplate or a woodscrew chuck can be used. There must of course be no gap where the bottom of the stem meets the base, so the latter must be shaped accordingly, and when cutting the pin on the end of the stem the bottom of the lamp can be slightly undercut to make sure of a neat job. The size of the pin is not critical, and most people seem to cut a pin of what seems a suitable size, then make the hole in the lamp base to fit. The alternative is to drill a hole of specific size in the base, and cut the pin to fit. If the former method is adopted, a tool known as a Columbus pattern vernier will be very helpful.

A hole will be required through the base, so that the flex can be run through and thence up the stem to the bulb holder, and the base should be drilled across the grain. This is a bench job, requiring a drill of suitable length and careful work to ensure that the hole is drilled radially to meet up neatly with the centre of the disc, emerging in the hole which accepts the stem. It is easier to run the wire through both pieces of the lamp before they are assembled.

Disaster quite often strikes lamps when they suffer a fall, and the bulb holder complete with brass nipple is torn from the wood. This should not happen, and the most commonly used form of nipple will give a very strong mounting. This is the short tubular variety which has a small diameter length threaded to go into the wood and a larger diameter length with an electrical thread to accept the bulb holder. An alternative, which does not give so much strength but looks very attractive, is a small brass disc with holes countersunk to take tiny screws and a section to take the bulb holder. These call for care in fitting, since to look really good they need to be recessed into the wood so that they lie flush. The screws are very small, and into end grain, so their grip is not really adequate, and some strong adhesive under the disc will help. The screws are of brass, and it is worth noting that where brass screws are used, steel ones of the same size should be inserted first, then removed. Brass screws are soft, and the tiny ones can easily break when being screwed home. A third type of nipple does exist, but is largely used on ceramic lamps and is not really suitable for wooden ones.

On occasions it may be found difficult to persuade the flex to pass through the stem of a lamp, particularly if it is a tall one. The process can be facilitated by using a piece of thin steel rod with its end cut square, prodding the wire as it is fed. Alternatively a length of steel rod, drilled through so that a nylon thread can be attached, can be dropped through first, like the 'pull-through' used to clean a rifle.

The thread can then be secured to the flex, and the rest is simple.

CANDLE HOLDERS

While most of us no longer creep upstairs to bed with a guttering candle like Wee Willie Winkie, the humble candle has made a come-back in a multitude of shapes and forms as a decorative feature, and there is still a need for candle holders, which are not a difficult project for a beginner. In my youth, which is now far distant, candles were of a certain size, and so the drilling of a hole in a candle holder was done with a drill bit of appropriate size. Nowadays, however, candles come in many shapes and diameters, and are frequently made as a minor 'craft' activity.

The difference between a candlestick and a candle holder is perhaps arguable, but in general the former is a taller object, designed for cylindrical candles, and is closely related to the traditional types of years ago. Candle holders are generally regarded as being shorter, and intended for use with the modern fat candles which form such colourful displays in the shops. The imagination of the turner can be given free rein here, since almost anything which will hold a candle safely, and is attractive, will do very well. Unfortunately, since the diameter of modern candles is not standardised, one has to provide a hole and let the eventual owner of the candle holder find a candle to fit. In this kind of project we have a situation similar to that which arises with table lamps, in that some candle holders can be made from one piece of wood, while others benefit from being made in two parts. In either case, however, the hole for the candle *must* be

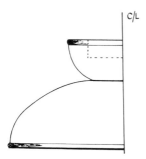

Simple design for candle holder.

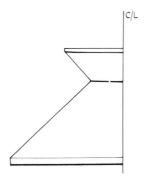

Design for candle holder, using tapers.

This procedure can be very useful, and is quite safe provided that the Jacobs chuck is firmly mounted. The turning, as in all projects, is based upon the basic cuts discussed in the earlier part of this book, all cuts being of a slicing nature, thus leaving the grain undisturbed.

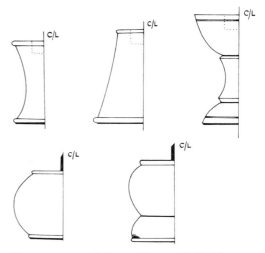

Some suggested shapes for candle holders.

central or the thing will look terrible. The longer versions of this sort of project will be made from square lengths of wood mounted between centres, and the candle hole will be drilled in the square blank before turning (the resulting hole can be plugged with a small tapered wooden plug if necessary) to provide easy access for the point of the tailstock centre. The 'short and fat' variety, often made from one piece of wood, will be turned without the use of the tailstock, using a woodscrew chuck, or an expanding collet type, and in such cases the hole can be drilled while the work is rotating on the lathe, feeding a suitable bit into the wood by means of the tailstock.

An idea which can have very attractive results is to turn objects from branch-wood, leaving a section at the base with bark still in place. This is particularly popular in the case of candle holders which are used for festive occasions such as Christmas or birthdays. The branch-wood selected should be fairly dry, and it is important to see that the bark is still firmly attached. If it is not, some may fly off during the turning, which could be dangerous, though naturally some form of eye protection should be used in all wood-turning and particularly when using the grinder. It is also disappointing if some of the bark falls away after the job is finished, so do inspect the timber carefully first. When the candle holder is completed, a coat or two of clear varnish will help to keep the bark from drying out and falling off.

10 Off-centre Turning

This is not a discussion of what happens if the work is put into the lathe off-centre by accident, but a brief look at one or two of the items which can be made by deliberately moving the wood off-centre. There are several uses for this technique, but most do not really belong in a beginner's guide. It is often necessary, however, to use this system in the making of tool handles, and I employ it when making toy wooden petrol tankers, either the road variety or tanker trucks for toy trains. Oval candle holders or table lamps are possible, and no doubt individual readers will think of their own applications.

Before I go on, I must point out that the shape produced is not strictly speaking an oval, it is ellipsoidal. I don't know the difference, nor indeed do I much care, but a mention of this fact may save some ink and postage for the compulsive letter-writers. Whatever you care to call it, the shape will certainly not be round, and I will stick to a loose usage of the expression 'oval'.

There is nothing unusual in the techniques of tool application in this branch of the craft, but it is necessary to have some knowledge of how to approach the matter of setting the job up. Rectangular sectioned blanks are often used, but square stuff can also be turned in this way. The techniques are slightly different. We can look at square stock first, and try the idea out on a fairly small piece of wood, say about $1\frac{1}{2}$ inches square and 8 inches long. This should be planed to a true square, either by hand or machine, and the ends cut with a sharp saw so that the diagonals can be carefully marked with a pencil to locate the true centres. With the pedant in mind, I must point out that the end of such a piece of wood can only have one centre, and that to speak of other centres is nonsense. Nevertheless, in this case it is customary to do so, the meaning being 'those points other than the true centre where the drive and/or tailstock centres will be positioned'.

Once the true centre has been marked at each end, the next move is to mark two

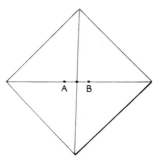

Marking-out procedure for oval turning using square stock.

92

points about ⅛ inch from each centre. These must be axially opposed, which means that the diagonals used should correspond. The sketch shows the idea. When the marking has been done, a small bradawl is pushed in at the relevant points to facilitate the mounting of the wood in the lathe.

The workpiece is mounted on its true centres and brought to a cylinder with the roughing gouge. The lathe is now stopped, and the work is repositioned on one of the pairs of off-centres. Check carefully to see that all clamps are tight, and rotate the lathe by hand to ascertain that the work will clear the toolrest. There will be some vibration with the blank running off-centre, but this should not cause any problems. If you are worried about it, drop the lathe speed a little. There is nothing dangerous about this operation, but the cutting may feel a little odd at first, since it is intermittent. It will be necessary to stop the lathe from time to time to check progress, and work should cease when half the wood has been dealt with. Now the blank is set up on the other pair of off-centre marks, and the other half of the job is done. Final sanding can be done by hand, or on the true centres in the lathe.

The marking out for rectangular stock is quite different, as can be seen in the

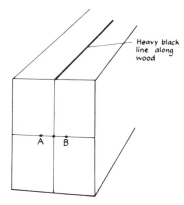

Heavy black line along wood

A   B

When rectangular stock is used the marking out is different.

sketch. The diagonals are not used, but the marking out takes the form of a cross and the intersection of the two lines must pass through the exact centre of the wood. The rest of the marking out will be quite obvious from the sketch, and the turning will be much as for the square. The use of heavy black pencil lines as guides should be noted, the turning being continued at each off-centre mounting until these are reached. Final sanding, if required, can again be done on the true centres, and I often use strips cut from sander belting, of a fine grade, looping this once round the job and holding an end in each hand.

11 Built-up Blanks

This is an almost infinite subject, about which it would be quite possible to write a long book. All I can do here is to introduce the basic idea for the consideration of beginners, who are likely to be very enthusiastic once their turning abilities have reached an adequate standard.

One thing must be made quite clear at the outset, this being that 'near enough' will not do in this kind of work. Sloppy workers will be well advised to leave it alone, since incompetent attempts can be frustrating and dangerous. Steady, careful work will produce very good results, with no more potential danger than would be present in any other form of turning, so don't let me put you off. This kind of lathe work calls for absolute precision at every stage, if satisfactory results are to be achieved, but it is not especially difficult. It is well worth taking as much care as possible over the centring of built-up blanks in the lathe, because even a tiny error will scream for attention in the finished job. The construction of the built-up blanks should also be done with extreme accuracy, so that the job does not fly apart in the lathe, and there are no glue lines in the finished job. One is intended to be able to see that the project has been made from a number of pieces of wood, even when. the same material is used throughout, but in good work the adhesive

itself does not show. This will only be so if the cutting of the pieces has been 100 per cent accurate, and any project should be abandoned if the fit of the segments is not absolutely correct. In view of all this I have never been tempted to buy any of the ready-made blanks often advertised in the woodworking press. They are probably very good, but the 'probably' worries me.

Most blanks used in built-up turning really call for the use of machinery if the high degree of accuracy required is to be achieved, though some very skilled woodworkers do make blanks with hand tools. Since my own woodturning is commercially orientated the time factor is of considerable importance, and I have to use machinery. Those who have a good quality circular saw, which is kept in exact adjustment, will have a great advantage, and the other machine which figures largely in this work is a planer/thicknesser, of the 'over-and-under' variety.

Given this sort of equipment, it is as well not to make up individual blanks, on a 'one off' basis, but to have sessions in which quantities of blanks of various kinds are produced, to be kept as stock for future turning. This will effect an enormous saving in time, and once the machines are set exactly for the job in hand, it makes sense to have a run at it. Certain

94

forms of blank, for example those in which bowls and similar items are turned from rings which are built up in segments, will be far easier if a good thicknesser is available, since it is vital that the thickness of the pieces in individual rings is the same.

I now use Cascamite or Aerolite as adhesives for this kind of work, in preference to the white polyvinyl acetates which have a tendency to 'creep' very slightly at the joints after the job is turned, spoiling the 'feel' of the finished item. They also rely upon the wood to draw the water from them in order to set. If the wood is damper than it should be, their efficiency seems to me to be reduced. The other adhesives I have mentioned are sometimes criticised in books for what appear to me to be silly reasons. It is said that they set very hard, and flying particles coming away during the turning could cause eye injury. So – wear goggles, or a visor. They are also said to take the edges off the tools, which they may well do, but not to any noticeable degree, and since it takes me about fifteen seconds to replace the edge on a gouge I am not impressed by this objection. In fact, these adhesives are formidably efficient, and entirely suitable for work of this nature.

POST-BLOCKED BLANKS

Perhaps one of the best ways to begin will be to examine the procedure for constructing what are known as 'post-blocked' blanks, which are popular for table lamps and can be used for other projects. These depend upon a perfectly square length of wood (the post) which must be prepared very carefully and centred in the lathe before any other part of the job is done. The ends are marked out very carefully in the normal way, by drawing in the diagonals to find the centres, but this should be done with a sharp pencil, preferably 6H. A hard pencil like this will produce a fine line, which helps with the accuracy.

A tiny bradawl mark is made at each end, and the blank can be mounted in the lathe, but *not* tightened. Just a single turn on the tailstock handwheel to nip the blank will do for the moment. The toolrest is now set up along the wood, so that the accuracy of the mounting can be checked and, if necessary, adjusted. A skew chisel, or a pencil, or something suitable, can be placed on the toolrest, and the wood is rotated by hand so that each corner of the square can be checked. This must be done at both ends of the wood, and if there is any discrepancy it should be very slight. Final adjustment, if required, can be made by thumping the blank in the appropriate direction with the fist, because the drive and tailstock centres are only just into the end grain of the wood, and the blank will move fairly easily. When all is satisfactory, the tailstock can be tightened fully, and a final check can be carried out. This is done by running a very narrow cut straight in at each end of the wood, using only the extreme corner of a parting tool. This produces a slightly raised circle on the end of the wood, the position of which in relation to the square can be evaluated with ease. All should be well, but if by chance it is not the blank should be rejected and saved for some other purpose.

When all is judged to be correct as regards centring, the tailstock is tightened so that the drive centre makes a clear mark on the end of the wood, and a small nick is made with a file in one of the fangs of the drive centre. A pencil mark is now made on the wood against the marked fang so that the blank can be returned to the lathe, after building up, in exactly the same orientation.

The use of a thicknesser helps a great deal in the preparation of truly square blanks, and these machines are worthwhile investments for woodturners. The procedure is to plane one side of a square length of wood, then plane an adjacent side with the first side firmly against the fence of the machine (which must be set exactly at 90 degrees to the table). When these two sides have been planed, producing a true right-angle, the wood is passed through the thicknesser twice, each time with one of the originally planed surfaces against the thicknesser table. The result of this will be a true square.

Building the Blanks

When a batch of posts has been produced and successfully centred, the building process can start, the first move being to surround each post along all or part of its length with contrasting timber. The thickness of this is a matter of individual choice, and it will be interesting to experiment, but the pieces used in building must be perfectly flat, with parallel faces, so once again the thicknesser will be a blessing. Hand tools can be used, but this is a slow process. Accuracy is of paramount importance, so the work must not be rushed. The first move is to fix a piece of prepared timber to two opposing sides of each blank, but don't try to use wood which is exactly the width of the post. It is more satisfactory to have the strips a little wider than the blanks, giving an 'overhang' which can be trimmed flush on a circular saw, as shown in the drawing.

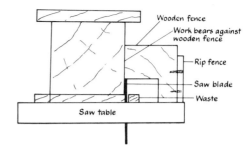

Removing overhangs on first pair of blocks.

When all the blanks have passed through this stage, and the adhesive has set, the overhangs are trimmed and the remaining two sides can be dealt with. The strips are wider now, covering both the post and the edges of the first two strips. There must be *no* gaps. Space will not permit detailed discussion, but this should get you going, and work of this kind is really a matter of common sense. As always, sharp tools should be used in the turning, and scrapers should be avoided as far as possible. It is also important not to be impatient. Work must be firmly cramped up in a warm room while the adhesive sets, sufficient time being allowed for this.

Turning Post-blocked Blanks

The turning of these blanks poses no special problems, but for those unaccustomed to built-up work the knack lies in knowing when to stop. The lathe should be switched off frequently so that progress can be inspected, and some thought should be given to the possible results of further cutting at specific points. This is an absorbing aspect of the craft, and it can be addictive.

BOWLS FROM 'BRICKS'

Another form of built-up work which has become very popular is the making of bowls from large numbers of tiny wooden 'bricks', using contrasting colours. Many other items can be made from blanks constructed along these lines, but here I will stick to bowls to reduce possible confusion. A common term for this kind of work is 'chequered turning', and although the cutting of the segments and building of the blanks is rather time-consuming, there are some advantages and the completed bowls can be very attractive. The length of time taken in building blanks is offset by two factors. First, beginners often have trouble with bowl-turning because of the grain structure which makes it difficult for them to obtain a really good finish. With bowls made as described here, however, the grain is running around the blank, and excellent finishes can be produced by quite inexperienced workers. Second, of course, the hollowing of a bowl takes time, especially in the early stages of a turner's career, and there are often problems of tool control. With these blanks there is little hollowing to do, and as the grain direction is favourable, those who are doubtful of their abilities with gouges can use sharp scrapers without greatly reducing the quality of the finish. Gouges, however, are very much faster in action than scrapers, and always cleaner-cutting if correctly used, so the scrapers should be abandoned once adequate gouge control has been achieved.

The production of blanks for any form of built-up turning is best done on a batch basis, sticking to a sensible system so that time is not wasted. In this 'brick-built' blank-making, complete accuracy is abso-lutely essential, and any completed brick blank about which the turner is doubtful should be rejected. The wastage of a small amount of timber and time is far better than injury resulting from an attempt to turn a sloppily built blank. No cracks, gaps, or glue lines can be permitted – the work has to be perfect to be 'near enough'!

One point which is often overlooked is that solid wooden bases for bowls like this are not suitable, because unless they are thoroughly coated with something which will protect them from atmospheric changes they may shrink or expand, and as this movement is greater across the grain than with it, the bowl can be broken. Many people use thick plywood discs, which are sufficiently stable for the purpose. A good cramping device, designed for use in the construction of brick-built bowls and some other forms of build-up, is a worthwhile investment. There are few available, but the leading craft suppliers will probably be able to help. Such cramps normally consist of a length of wide flexible steel, both ends of which fit into a handle which has a screw thread to tighten the cramp around the build-up.

Once the first two or three projects have been successfully completed with this form of construction, the beginner will realise that there is nothing difficult about it, and success is almost certain if the cutting and assembly of the components is really accurate. I would like to go into the subject deeply, but space restrictions must be observed, so I will give a broad picture which should suffice.

Preparing the Bricks

The first decision will be in respect of the number of bricks to be used in each ring, the number then being divided into 180 degrees to find the required angle. If, for example, we choose to have 18 bricks per ring, the angle will be 10 degrees. Whether the cutting is done by hand, using a fine backsaw and a home-made jig, or on a circular saw, the angle must be cut precisely. Remember that any error will be present twice in each brick, both ends having been cut, so an error of only 0.25 degrees will be 0.5 degrees per brick, giving an overall error in the ring of 9 degrees!

One little trick which is very helpful is to cut enough bricks for one ring, and to assemble them carefully in the cramp without any adhesive. When the cramp has been tightened – and don't screw it up until your face turns blue in the hope of closing gaps – the whole thing can be held up against a strong light for inspection. If there are inaccuracies, light will be seen through the joints, and the cutting jig must be corrected before going on.

Given the number of bricks per ring, the diameter of the bowl will depend upon their length, so it may help to draw the job out on paper or to cut some various lengths from scrap wood to establish the desired dimension. The material from which the bricks are cut should first be passed through a thicknesser, or thicknessed by hand planing. A variation of thickness in rings would not necessarily matter too much, but the blocks in each ring *must* be of equal thickness. For this reason the prepared wood should be cut into bricks as soon as possible, and those not immediately used should be sealed in plastic bags. Each bag is given a batch number, to prevent problems if the thicknesser has been used for other things between cutting sessions.

Any 'rag', or whiskers, left by the sawblade, should be removed with abrasive paper, but don't overdo this. A good tungsten carbide blade, if sharp, will leave little, and a fine-toothed crosscut pattern in ordinary carbon steel will do almost as good a job. There is no need to sand the ends of the blocks, since the sawn surface helps to give a 'key' for the adhesive.

Planning the Construction

Before starting on the first actual bowl it is advisable to experiment with patterns, using dry bricks, and making rows using varying widths of brick. The row which goes next to the base is often made wider to facilitate shaping. The building should be done on a flat sheet of metal, or any flat surface from which adhesive can be easily cleaned at the end of the building session. Blanks are usually built inverted in the cramp, the first row put in being the one which will form the top edge of the bowl.

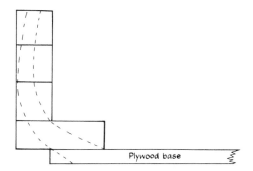

How bowl shape is obtained from the completed blank.

Excess glue squeezed out by the cramp will then drain out of the assembly rather than into it. There is no need to glue both ends of the bricks, or to use masses of adhesive, but all contact surfaces should be fully covered. When the first ring is in, it can be spread with adhesive, ready to receive the next. The final ring, or top ring since we are building the blank upside-down, will be made up of wider bricks, to be glued to the base. Three or four layers of bricks can be fitted into the cramp, according to timber thickness, but deep bowls can be made by gluing two blanks together under pressure. The second blank in such cases will have no layer of wide bricks.

The Base

The base, preferably of ½-inch plywood, should be marked out with compasses or a pair of dividers so that there will be a clear indication of the centre, then cut out on the bandsaw or with a coping saw, and if the result is a bit rough the disc can be mounted on a faceplate and trimmed to a true circle. The bonding agents used in plywood are rough on tool edges, but by this time sharpening should be no problem. When the disc is ready it can be glued to the blank, but great care must be taken in centring it, for obvious reasons. It could now be left while the adhesive sets, with a heavy weight on it, but this ties up the cramp and puts a stop to the building session. The answer here is to make up some cramping jigs (again some ½-inch plywood will be useful). These are simply discs with holes drilled through their centres to accept stout bolts with washers and wing nuts. When the job has been cramped up in one of these, the flexible cramping jig can be removed and work can start on the next blank. Note that when this method is used the fitting of the base will have to be done later.

Turning the Bowl

The discs used as cramping jigs should have newspaper or thick brown paper between them and the wood so that they do not become permanently attached by stray adhesive, and when the first blank is ready for turning it may look a little on the scruffy side. Don't worry about this; most built-up blanks have this sort of appearance before turning, but if the assembly has been accurate, and the turning is done well, they will look magnificent when they are completed. In this sort of assembly the grain runs round the blank, so there are no end grain problems, and the turning is in some respects much easier for a beginner than is the case with a solid blank. A sharp round-nosed scraper could be used for the whole job, but scrapers are only a substitute for cutting tools, and the idea is to become a woodturner, so it is better to cut the job with the ⅜-inch deep-fluted gouge. Some books suggest that scrapers should be used exclusively for all built-up work, on the grounds that they are safer, but beginners can have accidents with them if they do not understand the finer points of tool use, and one of the most serious accidents possible in turning can arise when scrapers are pointed upwards inside bowls. Do *not* stand in line with the edge of work on a faceplate, particularly built-up jobs. With modern adhesives and accurate building there should be no chance of the assembly self-destructing, but stand out of line while turning, and keep spectators to one side. If the bowl is very large, the speed will need to be low, and it is advisable for beginners to turn all built-up blanks fairly slowly. Again, run the lathe at a speed where you feel comfortable.

The outside turning will be quite

straightforward, but there is a little more difficulty when shaping the inside. It is obviously necessary to blend the bowl wall with the base, without cutting into the plywood disc which must not happen or the job will be spoiled. For this reason you may like to join wall and base by means of a tiny step cut with the corner of a sharp scraper, but take care not to cut into the base.

CONSTRUCTIONS

There are so many types of construction, and so many possible combinations of these into blanks, that the subject seems almost limitless, and I have space here only to indicate a few of the better known and most useful approaches. With a little thought, individual turners can produce ideas of their own, but the chances of coming up with something new are now remote. One simple and very useful construction for what are often referred to as 'box blanks', suitable for biscuits or perhaps to hold the marmalade jar at breakfast, is the building-up of solid rings on a disc base. The rings can be of various timbers to give contrast, and their grain should be alternated in the build-up to give stability. The rings are easily cut with a coping saw, but I find the little Hegner powered fretsaws invaluable for this, and for many other jobs in the workshop.

It is often said that woods used in built-up work should be of similar hardness, to avoid the problem of tools cutting more deeply into the softer woods. There is, in my view, no sound basis for this if the turner is competent, and I frequently combine softwoods with quite hard timbers. One should practise until a high degree of tool control has been achieved,

rather than try to find ways of avoiding the need for it.

One problem which does arise with work in which different woods are combined is discoloration of the lighter timbers by the darker ones when sanding. For this reason, tool work should be of the highest order, using sharp edges, and if abrasive paper really must be used the process should be kept to a minimum.

'Sidestack' Blank

The 'sidestack' is a useful sort of blank, and is very easily made without the need to cut awkward angles. It consists of a number of strips of wood, say 2 inches by 1 inch, and 12 inches or so long, glued together side by side, with the pieces on edge. This will produce a flat build-up 2 inches thick, which is striped. From this a disc can be cut, but care is needed to place the centre so that the resulting disc is properly in balance as regards its appearance. These discs can be constructed quite quickly, and will make interesting bowls. Strips of good-quality pine (if you can find any) can be glued together to form flat, edge-jointed boards about a foot square, which are then planed truly flat and built up so that each section has its strips running at 90 degrees to the sections above and below. A disc cut from a construction like this will produce excellent results provided that the turner has reached a stage of competence which permits satisfactory turning in this rather demanding wood.

Pie Wedge Blank

The 'pie wedge' blank is very popular for dishes, and for bases to fit to built-up lamp stems and the like. The name is al-

Built-up base for a standard lamp, using a variety of timbers.

most self-explanatory, in that the build-up looks like a pie which has been cut ready for serving. These wedges are crosscut from boards, therefore the grain runs across them and so round the blank, making it easy to turn. Experience has made me cautious about mentioning brand names for some items, since they often disappear from the market soon after a book is published, but high street shops such as Halfords stock a variety of items which can be of great value in the turner's shop. I am referring now to devices intended for cramping circular objects, many of those in the shops being meant for the large-diameter trunking used in air conditioning systems. Most of these come with continuous lengths of special metal strapping, and a number of small tightening devices, and they can be cut to length to suit any normal build-up. There are also some plastic versions which work very well and can be joined to each other to give the size required.

Spacers and Wedges

Spacers can be inserted in built-up blanks,

and the thickness can be varied. Sometimes thin veneer is used, and if this is of a contrasting colour to the blank the results are quite pleasing. Note that the use of spacers produces a hole at the centre of a wedge blank. Oil-tempered hardboard can be used for spacers, and when the turned article has been polished this becomes very dark and is most effective. The cheaper forms of hardboard should not be used.

Odd effects can be achieved by angle-cutting the wedges, crosscutting them from a bevel-ripped strip with the saw table slightly tilted. Bevel-ripped strips are triangular in section, and usually cut about 2 feet long for convenience. They are ripped from the edge of a plank with the saw table tilted, the wood being turned over after each cut. The use of such wedges gives the built-up disc a spiral appearance on its edge. If a spiral effect is required on the face of the disc, the blank is made up from right-angled triangles. In this case, the points of the sections will not run to the centre of the assembly, as is normal, but will form a hole at the centre due to the spacers, and the hypotenuse of each triangle will run at a tangent to the hole. If these triangles are bevel-ripped, and crosscut to the desired width, the blank will have end grain on its faces. If, however, they are produced by crosscutting from a suitable board, the grain will run round the blank.

FALSE COOPERING

I regret being unable to continue at length on this subject because it is one in which I have always been very interested, but I will include some pointers on the aspect of built-up work known as 'false coopering'.

The magnificent grain of yew, together with its rich colours, gives an extremely attractive mug or tankard, built from eight staves.

This is one of my favourite techniques, and I use it mainly in the production of tankards. These, with a suitably shaped handle which has been neatly fitted, can look very attractive, and they are uncommon. They make excellent gifts, and always seem to be readily saleable. The term 'false coopering' is used because these blanks, like barrels, are made up of staves, and indeed excellent small barrels can be made in this way. The process is not true coopering, because the staves are turned to a curved shape rather than bent as in the making of large barrels.

Preparing the Blanks

As with other forms of blanks built by the turner, the need for extreme accuracy in the cutting of the sections, or in this case staves, cannot be over-emphasised. Safety is paramount, but it is also important to have no heavy glue lines at the joints, which are unsightly and a sure sign of a sloppy worker. The number of staves in a blank of this kind is a matter of choice, but I tend to use eight staves in tankard blanks, and the result is pleasing. The angle at the corners of a four-sided construction like a picture frame is 45 degrees, as most people are aware, and very much so if they have tried making the things. With an eight-sided blank like the one for our tankard, the angle will therefore be 22.5 degrees – *exactly*.

The staves are usually cut in fairly long lengths, for ease of working, and with a really sharp sawblade the resulting finish will do for the construction. Alternatively the staves can be cut initially with a rectangular section, the required angle being put on by means of a planer with its fence tilted to the necessary angle. Before embarking on mass production, it will be well worth while to draw some circles on paper, divide them accurately into eight, ten, or twelve sections, then draw lines to show the end view of a construction. This will establish the width and thickness of the staves for a specific project.

The blanks can either be assembled from the long staves, which is rather tricky, or the staves can be cut to length

Metal strapping used on 'coopered' work, showing tightening device.

before assembly, which I prefer to do. They are then glued up and set aside for a while until the adhesive is thoroughly set. Individual turners have their own ways of setting up and shaping these blanks, and I am not suggesting that the method I use is the best, merely that I have used it for many years and found it satisfactory.

Mounting and Shaping

When the blanks are ready, the next move is to prepare them for mounting in the lathe, and a little thought here will pay dividends. Some turners fit a disc to one end of the blank, mount the assembly on the lathe, and go ahead with the turning. The job *can* be done this way, but there are certain inherent difficulties. The problems arise in the shaping of the inside, and there is a high risk of ruining the project unless the turner is very highly skilled.

One snag when working inside objects of this kind is that the waste removed has no means of escape, so that the blank rapidly fills with shavings which have to be removed frequently, by stopping the lathe and raking them out. This is fine, except that some are always present, preventing observation of the cut at the bottom of the hole, and it is not easy to shape the inside wall without catching the scraper in the base of the job, which may completely ruin it. There is also considerable overhang of the tool from the toolrest, which aggravates any dig-in. It helps if the toolrest can be turned so that it projects into the bowl, but then the support at the bottom of the hollow is on the extreme end of the toolrest, which may provoke some flexing.

The system I use is outlined here, and does help a great deal with these prob-

lems, though I have only been using it for the last eight or nine years. I take a disc of wood about 1 inch thick, and mount it on a woodscrew chuck or an expanding collet. I then cut a rebate on the front of the disc, working carefully until the raised part of the disc will just enter the end of the blank. The disc is then taken from the lathe and glued in place. Normally I would do a dozen or so blanks as a batch. When the adhesive has set, I remount the assembly on the lathe and shape the inside, working down to an inch or two from the bottom and leaving the rest untouched. Having gone as far as I can with this process, I set the toolrest up across the front of the job and cut a rebate on the inner edge of the wall. The blank is then removed, and a disc of wood for the base is mounted and rebated to be a push fit into the blank. This is glued up and allowed to set, whereupon I cut off the end of the blank which has the first disc fixed to it, usually sawing it off on the bandsaw.

The job now has a base which marries up neatly with the wall, and all that remains is to finish shaping the inside, the

A tankard in burr elm, nearly completed.

Some stages in 'coopering'. *Left to right:* octagonal beech blank; tankard in ash; mug in yew.

part which was left untouched now being at the front. This is quite easy, and since I adopted this procedure I have had no failures. Because the base has been carefully fitted as a push fit, the blank is running true, and the job is soon over. Scrapers have to be used inside these projects, which is a pity, so there will be a need for some abrasive paper. Be warned, however, that with this sort of work it can be dangerous to put a hand inside when sanding. The best way is to wrap some foam-rubber sheet round a cylinder of wood, and wrap abrasive paper round that. The sanding can then be carried out in safety.

Handles

Handles for tankards can be cut out with a fretsaw from suitable stock, and shaped by hand carving and sanding. They are best attached to the tankard by means of small tenons cut on their ends and fixed

with Araldite into tiny mortises cut in the body of the job. This operation must not be rushed, or the job may be spoiled. I never use polyurethanes for this work, but always finish receptacles of this kind with one of the two-part catalyst resins, which resist hot liquids and mild acids.

Many beginners who have acquired some turning skill complain that they cannot 'think of shapes'. This is quite natural in the early days, but there are plenty of artefacts in the home or in shops which will provide basic ideas. The shapes need not necessarily be copied, but they can be used as starting points and modified to individual taste. Do be quite sure that you have mastered the tools by practising the basic cuts before worrying about this sort of thing, or life will be difficult because your mind is divided between tool manipulation and shaping. Eventually the tools will feel like extensions of the arms, and the right movements will be instinctive.

12 Timber Types and Finishing Methods

TIMBER TYPES

It would be possible to provide a very long list of woods, since almost all varieties of timber can be used, but this information is available from other sources and there are books which deal exclusively with it. All I can do here is provide a short list of easily obtainable types to help beginners with their choice. I am frequently asked, 'What is the best wood for turning?' but there is no real answer to this. If one is looking for wild grain and lots of colour, yew will take some beating. Beech is commonly and traditionally used for furniture, sycamore for kitchen utensils, and so on, but there are no hard and fast rules. It is important for beginners to try all the sound pieces of wood they can get their hands on, and to make their own decisions as to their favourites. In the hope that it may be of some assistance, I have included the following brief guide.

Oak Open-grained, hard, and expensive if of good quality. This is a favourite with me for small furniture.

Beech Normally uninteresting as regards grain, but turns very easily and finishes well. Kiln-dried beech is fairly easy to obtain, and I turn a lot of it in the course of making toys.

Sycamore A very light-coloured wood. The grain is not striking, but the timber is fairly soft and easy to turn. I use it in built-up blanks quite often.

Ash Another favourite, has stronger grain than sycamore, and pleasant pinkish colour. Turns well, and can be used for a wide variety of projects.

Sweet chestnut Often mistaken for oak, and is a good choice for beginners if available locally.

Lime Much favoured by carvers, being soft and easy to carve. It resembles sycamore, and is another wood used in built-up turning.

Holly Almost white in colour, so is used for laminating and building blanks. An excellent contrast against dark timbers such as walnut, and easy to turn.

Cherry This can turn extremely well, and often has a pleasing greenish hue. Usually available as logs from a garden, but these have the central heart in them and the finished project may subsequently split.

Apple All the fruit woods are pleasant to turn and I have included apple in this list because, alphabetically speaking, it comes first. Napkin rings are often made from branchwood from fruit trees because they can be made from wood which is still quite wet. Only a ring at the outer part of the branch actually remains, and this dries evenly.

Box Now very expensive, but a delight to turn. When it is not quite bone dry, shavings will stream from it like string, giving the beginner's ego a tremendous boost. It is available only in the form of 'billets', which are small-diameter pieces with the bark on.

Elm Beautiful when the turning has been done and the polish applied, but many people, myself included, need to wear a mask when turning it dry as the dust can be very upsetting to the eyes, nose and throat. To me the smell is also unpleasant, though this is subjective and many may like it. Not a stable timber, and likely to move after the job is finished.

Pine Pine is a softwood, which means that it comes from a tree which does not shed its leaves in the autumn – in other words a coniferous tree. A hardwood comes from a tree which is deciduous, meaning that it does shed its leaves, but the division of woods in this way is ridiculous, since balsa is one of the softest woods in the world and is by this system of classification a hardwood, whereas yew is extremely hard but retains its leaves in winter, and so is a softwood. Good pine turns well if sharp tools and correct methods are used, but is considered non-turnable by many who have never properly mastered the craft.

FINISHING METHODS

This is another subject which could easily fill a fair-sized book, and I can only outline some of the more common finishing methods here. These, however, should be more than enough to keep new turners going for quite a while.

There is one point which must be made clear at the outset, this being that in any form of woodwork, no finishing material or method can produce top quality results unless the wood is in as perfect a condition as possible before the finishing process begins. I am often asked how 'professional' finishes are obtained in woodturning, and I am afraid the answer must be that the top woodturners achieve better results than those less skilled simply because the quality of their turning is higher. 'How did you get that finish?' is a common question, but I fear there is no magic potion which can be applied to a mangled and bedraggled piece of wood with any hope of transforming it into a beautiful piece of work. One cannot polish a doormat, but a tiled floor can be brought to a magnificent sheen. We have therefore to use every bit of skill available during the turning if we want a beautiful finish.

Relatively few finishing materials are in common use by woodturners, and the main points concerning these are covered here. Most are very easy to use, but those using them for the first time would be well advised to turn up some cylinders between centres and try them out before applying them to important projects.

Abrasive Paper

Assuming first-class tool work throughout the job, some abrasive paper will often be needed on bowls and other forms of disc, but it should be avoided entirely between centres. When spindle-turnings are sanded, the abrasive particles are crossing the grain, and quite deep scratches may result. These are extremely difficult to remove and their presence will ruin the job.

Many examples of this sort of thing can be observed in craft shops which buy in articles made by amateur turners. If these scratches are present, the finishing processes will not hide them but will act as a 'lens', bringing the faults into sharp focus. If abrasive paper must be used, it should be as fine as possible, and I would not normally think of using anything coarser than grade 320 between centres. Even then the abrasive work would be limited to a period of two minutes or so. Bowls, and other forms of disc, will need sanding, and slightly coarser paper can be used initially, finishing with fine grades.

Some workers fit switches which reverse the rotation of the motor, so that when the fibres of the wood have been pushed in one direction by the abrasive paper, the lathe can be reversed, improving the effect of the sanding. This can be dangerous, and in my view is best avoided, since the idea is really only of use to those who ought to be practising to improve their techniques of cutting. The fact is that faceplates and chucks, like the nuts which hold car wheels, are self-locking in normal use. If the lathe is run in reverse it is possible for the work, complete with chuck or faceplate, to be flung from the machine, with the possibility of injury to the turner. If this reversing idea must be adopted, some positive provision should be made for locking the faceplate or chuck so that it cannot unscrew itself.

One other point on safety, which really should not need stating, is that it is possible to run into one danger while trying to avoid another. I was recently asked to review a book on woodturning in which the author was shown wearing what appeared to be gardening gloves, which he said protected his hands from splinters. One is forced to wonder why it is necessary to have one's hands in contact with the wood while turning, and what kind of surface finishes are being produced if splinters are being dispensed so freely. After more than forty years in this craft, I have to state what I have had no problems with splinters, and I would not wear gloves while turning even if offered good money to do so. What might happen if a glove became trapped between the work and the toolrest I will leave to your imagination.

One last point with regard to sanding – do avoid altogether the sanding of fine detail, which is almost inevitably affected adversely by the process. If it has been cut properly it will not require abrasives, and if it has not, they will be of little help. I once read a letter in a woodworking magazine in which the writer said that he had been taught how to sand detail, but one wonders at the quality of tuition which suggests the need for such action.

Beeswax

Writings on this craft make frequent references to beeswax as a polish, but in fact it is used more as a filler, followed by a smear of high-quality polishing wax, such as 'Antiquax', which is intended for valuable furniture. Beeswax is available in two forms, either in its natural state, when it has a dark colour, or as a refined product, which is pale yellow. The former is fine on dark woods, but the refined form is better for the light ones. The application of beeswax in woodturning could hardly be simpler, and it involves none of the hard work which faces the unfortunate cabinet-maker.

When the wood is ready for treatment, a scrap of beeswax is applied to it as it revolves, moving along the job so that all the surface is covered. A piece of soft dry rag, folded to protect the turner's fingers from the frictional heat, is then pressed firmly on to the surface and moved around to melt the wax and distribute it evenly. Excess wax is removed by the cloth, and awkward corners can be dealt with by folding the rag so that a fine edge is produced. When using cloths for polishing extreme care should be exercised to preclude any possibility of their being 'grabbed' by the rotating wood, or by the lathe centres. All cloth which is not being rubbed on to the wood should be folded into the palm of the hand. The finish produced by beeswax alone is attractive, and is fine on some timbers, such as oak. If a high polish is needed, however, a polishing wax will be applied, and some turners find that increasing the lathe speed improves the result.

Two-part Catalyst Resin

When considering the finish to be applied to a project, its functional aspect must receive attention. An article which will not be handled constantly or need to be washed, can be waxed. Items such as sugar bowls, pepper mills, or tableware such as wooden plates, must have some other treatment. Polyurethanes are often used, but I gave them up many years ago in favour of the two-part catalyst resins which I mentioned earlier. These harden by chemical action after they have been mixed and applied, as distinct from 'drying', and they offer a high degree of protection for objects which are frequently handled or need to be washed. They are proof against boiling water, burning cigarettes, mild acids, and (almost) children.

These substances must be used according to the instructions provided by their manufacturers, and their main disadvantage is that a foul smell is produced as they harden. This does not persist, I am happy to say, but it is not a good idea to use the stuff indoors unless you have a very tolerant family. The workshop is not the best place either, as there is always some dust where abrasives are used. They must be mixed in ceramic or glass jars, not in metal or plastic containers, as the acid hardener will attack metal and some plastics. Rubber gloves should be worn to protect the hands, and some eye protection is advisable, just in case.

I normally give one, or sometimes two coats of this substance, followed by a coat of thinned mixture. Thinners of a special kind can be purchased for these resins, as can brush-cleaning fluid. Once the resin has hardened on the wood it can be polished to a magnificent shine with a special paste, available from the makers, or with silver polish on a rag. If a matt finish is desired, fine steel wool can be passed lightly over the job.

Friction Polish

Certain substances known as 'friction polishes' can be obtained, though they seem to me to be suspiciously similar to the old 'button polish' which was so popular at one time. They are shellac based, with other ingredients which are unspecified, and if used correctly they will produce a good shine. This surface is not, however, durable, and so is unsuitable for some work. It will not like moisture, nor will it appreciate frequent handling, and some form of sanding sealer, which I will discuss shortly, must be used first. If a friction polish is to be used, one must remember that it is very much akin to a French polish, and so should be applied by means of a 'rubber'. This is a folded piece of soft cloth wrapped around a ball of cotton wool. The polish is poured over the cotton wool, and passes through the cloth to the wood. Results obtained by using only the cloth, to which the polish has been applied direct, will be inferior. It is also worthy of note that these polishes are what I describe as 'diameter conscious', in that the surface speed of a point on a workpiece which is being driven at a constant speed depends upon the diameter of the wood at that point. This being so, practice is needed to obtain the best results with friction polishes because the pressure used with the rubber needs to be varied so that it relates to the surface speed. More pressure will be required on small diameters than on large ones. Once the knack has been acquired, however, this adjustment of pressure becomes automatic. Note that immediately after use the rubber should be popped into a jar or some container which has a fairly tight-fitting lid. If it is left on the bench it will become as hard as a rock in a short time.

One safety point which must be mentioned is that all rags used for polishing should be removed from the workshop at the end of the day, and preferably burned. Some substances used in finishing are capable of causing spontaneous combustion under certain conditions, and heaps of discarded rag can begin to smoulder. I have never known this to happen, but learned men of scientific bent assure me that it is possible.

Sanding Sealer

I mentioned sanding sealers, and it is necessary for the importance of these substances to be appreciated. The most common forms are clear cellulose lacquer, and shellac. They may come with brand names, and other things may be mixed with them, but the basic substances will do the job, and clear cellulose is easy enough to obtain. The idea is to seal the surface of the wood so that polishes will remain on the surface rather than be driven into the wood, which will occur to a considerable extent on end grain which has not been sealed. It is this which produces the 'beginner's bowl', with two shiny areas and two rough areas. The more the thing is polished, if no sealer has been used, the worse it seems to get. The other purpose of sealer is to raise the grain of the wood, as a cabinet-maker does by applying water and letting it dry. The sealer does rather more than the water, because it raises the grain and locks it in the raised condition as it dries. Subsequent sanding then produces a smooth surface. Sealers can be somewhat volatile, and the maker's instructions should be observed. Don't dangle your cigarette over the mouth of a tin of cellulose, for example.

Sealers can be applied by means of a brush, or with a rag, either when the work is stationary or during rotation. The speed should be kept as low as possible in the latter case, however, or the stuff will fly everywhere and if the turner stands in the wrong place there will be no need for hair lacquer for a month or two.

Wood Stain

Woodturners do not use stains a great deal, but it may sometimes be necessary to employ them when repairing old furniture, or their use may be called for in a job which is brought in by a customer. For some reason I have a bad feeling about staining wood, though I do it if I have to. My feelings may perhaps be seen as irrational, but it seems a shame to change the natural colour and beauty of timber by means of chemicals. It is sometimes suggested that staining should be carried out before any sealer is applied, but I find that this can cause problems when water- or naptha-based stains are used because they rush into the end grain areas and make them very dark. I therefore like to put on a thin coat of sealer and sand the job with fine paper before staining. This inhibits the absorption of the stain and reduces the problem. An excellent range of stains and coloured polishes is now marketed in this country by a company called Liberon, and I recently acted in a consultant capacity for the firm, testing their products in my workshop. As a result, I now use these finishing materials, and find them most satisfactory.

Oil

Various oils are also used by turners, and a few comments on this subject may help. Teak oil is often referred to, but this is not easy to apply, tending to leave a slightly tacky surface which attracts dust. If it is applied with sufficient skill, the results are fine, but I prefer to use Danish oil in most cases, this being a mixture of thin oils which is far easier to apply and which gives consistently high-quality finishes. It is particularly effective as a finish on small oak furniture, which is one of the facets of the craft to which I am attracted. The oil has a pleasant odour, and is applied with a folded cloth as the work rotates. A series of thin coats is applied, with the lathe running fairly fast, and firm pressure is used on the cloth. Each coat is burnished until dry by means of a clean piece of soft dry cloth, and the end result is excellent.

On a recent demonstration tour in the mid-west of America I was introduced to a substance known as Tung oil. This seems not to be available in England, or rather I have been unable to locate a source, but it is effective, and I would place it somewhere between the two I mentioned earlier. It certainly does a good job, and I would have liked to have used it over a longer period in order to arrive at more definite conclusions, but it may appear in this country, and I would recommend a trial.

The finishes I have described should be sufficient to keep most beginners going for a while, but experiments should be carried out with any substances considered potentially viable for use in lathe work. It is worth noting that compatibility of substances used in finishing is essential. Some products will be found to have undesirable reactions when brought into contact with others, and the best way to avoid problems of this kind is to stick as far as possible to a range of products from one maker. In the event of any of these being incompatible, the fact will be clearly stated. If in doubt about the propriety of mixing two substances, the answer of course is to carry out some tests on scrap wood.

In my very early days I was inclined to apply self-adhesive green baize to far too many turned items. This is fine for objects such as plinths for sporting cups and so on, which are rarely handled, but a good piece of turning can look quite grim when its green baize has deteriorated. It is obviously no use on articles which will need to be washed, and I would suggest that it be employed with restraint.

13 Further Simple Projects

One or two items at various stages of turning are shown in the illustrations, without relevant text to describe the processes involved. This is because the basic techniques covered in the beginning of the book are applicable, and those who wish to tackle projects of this kind should be quite capable of doing so when preceding chapters have received sufficient study. I have, however, saved for the end of the book one or two interesting little projects which are suitable for beginners in that they can attempt them with a reasonable chance of producing a worthwhile article, and without meeting any insuperable problems.

Some of these projects involve the use of items which can easily be obtained from suppliers who advertise in the woodworking magazines, and the results can be very good if the job is not rushed and the tool techniques are correct. I have never seen a 'born woodturner', nor do I believe in the existence of such a phenomenon. The craft can be mastered by a combination of the application of acquired knowledge and determination, the latter being the essential ingredient. If woodturning were easy, it would attract far fewer people since most of us are looking for a challenge. In the early stages there will be failures, but there will also be successes.

Failures are frustrating, but will become less frequent as time passes. Successes produce a state of euphoria, and are well worth waiting for. Nothing is perfect, however, and the turner, like any other craftsman, must be his or her own critic. Women are now taking to the craft much more than was the case a few years ago, and they can become highly skilled. It seems to me that they are in general more artistic than men, and have a good eye for proportion in design. My own wife is now well on the road to becoming a competent woodturner, and may perhaps do some instructing herself in years to come.

This is a very pleasant hobby, having a high therapeutic value. The wood itself is a pleasure, surely one of the most beautiful natural materials, and woodturning satisfies the creative urge that lies within all human beings. It is also pleasant to think of leaving behind in this world some mark of one's presence in the form of objects which will give pleasure. They may even inspire future woodturners, which is an interesting thought.

In conclusion, then, a few projects. All are relatively simple, some a little more demanding than others, but careful work should produce encouraging results.

TOOL HANDLES

There seems to be a tendency among beginners to be fascinated by the turning of handles for woodturning tools, and this is a simple enough operation. I have no interest in handles, as long as they are not working themselves loose from the tang of the tool. My interest is in the blade, and only the part of that which does the work. Tool handles, unlike blades, do not wear out, nor do they normally break, so the need for a replacement is likely to be rare. It is possible, however, to buy just two or three tools to start out with, and to purchase others on a 'blade only' basis, and in this case the operation of turning a handle as described here will be worthwhile.

Handles for turning tools are made from square lengths of wood, the dimensions of which will be to suit the individual turner. There are no rules about tool handle sizes, but it is generally accepted that the longer blades have longer handles. Many turners like the gouges which they use for bowl work to have extra length in the handles so that they can be steadied against the hip.

It will be necessary to drill a hole to accept the 'tang' of the blade, and in fact because the tang is tapered two holes are drilled into the end of the wood, the second smaller than the first. This operation is carried out while the blank is still square. The drilling can be done in the lathe, using a Jacobs pattern chuck in the headstock with suitable bits, and pushing the square blank on to the rotating cutter by means of the tailstock. The hole in the end of the wood is not large, so the tailstock centre can run in it while the job is turned. If a small dead centre is used, the piece of metal tubing which will form the ferrule can be hung on it while the turning is done, so that it can be tried for fit on the turned pin without taking the job from the lathe. Allowance is made for a small piece of waste wood to be left at the headstock end, which will be cut away when

the turning is completed, leaving no drive centre mark.

The blank is first run down to a cylinder with the roughing gouge, in the normal manner, and some shape can be put into it with the same tool. The parting tool will be used at the drilled end to cut the pin, which will have dimensions to suit the ferrule. If, when the pin has been cut, it is found to be a slightly loose fit, not to worry; it will be tight enough once the handle has been fitted. I make a mark near the headstock end of the job, and roll a skew chisel point into this from alternate sides to form a curved V, then finish the shaping of the handle with a sharp spindle gouge, but I leave the V-cut shallow until this has been done. There should be no need for abrasive paper, but if there is it can be used now, and if the ferrule is a fairly good fit it can be polished up with emery paper as the work rotates. Finally the V-cut is deepened until the work begins to tremble a little (or the turner does) and the lathe is stopped. The job can now

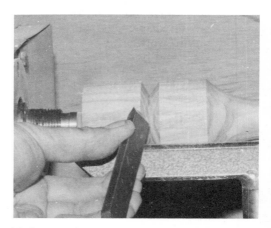

V-shapes should not be scraped, but cut cleanly with a chisel point. Only the extreme point may safely touch the wood.

be removed from the lathe, and the small waste piece is cut off with a fine saw. The sawn area can be sanded by hand. The best way to fit a blade is to push it firmly into the handle and then, with the blade pointing away from the body, strike the end of the handle hard with a mallet or block of wood. A couple of blows will do it, and it is surprising how tightly a handle will fit after this treatment which relies upon relative inertia of blade and handle. Any sound timber will do for handles, but ash and beech are often used.

CLOCK OR BAROMETER CASE

The next project involves the turning of a thick disc of wood into which a barometer of the aneroid variety will be fitted. The same procedure would of course be adopted in the making of a circular case for a wall clock. Basically this is just a matter of making a hole of suitable size in the blank to accept the barometer or clock mechanism, and shaping the remainder of the wood. I have not put forward any suggestions on shape: this will be a good opportunity to work out something pleasing on paper and have a try at it. Beware of letting the imagination run riot. It will be as well at this stage to stick to simple lines, which often look better on a small object and will not raise awkward problems.

Having obtained a barometer from one of the various specialist suppliers to the woodturning market, a piece of choice timber of suitable dimensions can be selected. The barometer mechanisms usually have a brass-type bezel, or rim, which looks very nice against dark or light timbers.

Choice of mounting device for this pro-

ject will be between faceplate, large wood-screw chuck and expanding collet. Any of these will do, but make sure that the job is firmly held. The toolrest is set up across the edge of the disc, which is then reduced in diameter with the $\frac{3}{8}$-inch deep-fluted

Barometer case at an early stage, the area to be recessed for the mechanism marked in pencil.

The barometer mechanism is a snug fit, and can be removed for final shaping and finishing of the case.

gouge, the tool used in all disc work. Keep the handle low and dictate the depth of cut to the tool. Never let the tool decide how much wood it will take off. When the disc is down to a true circle, the toolrest is moved round across the front of the job, and the area to be recessed is marked out carefully with a pair of dividers. One approach to the removal of the waste from this area is to bore a hole an inch or so wide to the depth required, and subsequently to enlarge this hole by means of the gouge, finishing up with a square-ended scraper.

Remember to make the hole a fraction too small in diameter at first, so that it can be enlarged carefully to achieve a fit. The timber used must be dry, since any shrinkage could damage the barometer and would certainly jam it in place for-ever. Unless some strange convoluted shape has been chosen, the whole of the work will be done with the disc-turning gouge, refreshing its edge on the grinder whenever judged necessary. Beginners often ask me how they are supposed to know when tools need sharpening, the answer to which is 'when in doubt, sharpen'.

Some sanding may be required, though not much, and when this has been done the selected finish can be applied, not for-getting the sanding sealer stage, of course. Access must be provided for the adjusting screw which will be found on the back of these barometers, and which allows them to be set according to the height above sea-level at which they are used. This can be by drilling a hole through from the back, or by taking the whole of the re-cessed area right through the job, leaving the back open. Another small hole can be drilled to enable the barometer to be hung on a nail, and the job is done.

BISCUIT-AND-CHEESE BOARD

A board to hold cheese or butter, with a trough for biscuits, makes a good project for newcomers to the craft, and the mak-ing of this is not a lengthy process. If de-sired, the trough could be replaced by a larger tile, so that the finished item could be used for cheese only.

A colourful ceramic tile let into a nicely turned and polished disc can be used as a cheese or butter server.

The diameter of the disc is not critical, and the thickness could be about an inch. As with the barometer case, the first operation is the trimming of the edge to a true circle, followed by the recessing of the centre of the wood to accept a small decorative tile. The recess for the tile is a simple job, and the parting tool will do well. The area is marked out, and a cut made at its outer edge to the required length. Further parting tool cuts, moving towards the centre each time, will provide a recess, and roughness in the bottom of it will not matter unduly. The tile is tried

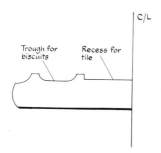

C/L

Trough for biscuits

Recess for tile

Cheese and biscuit platter.

disc gouge and if necessary finishing the shape with a sharp round-nosed scraper. The shaping or rounding-over of the edge comes next, and one should bear in mind that the board has to be picked up from the table. It is therefore tapered away at the bottom to provide a finger grip. If a large expanding collet chuck has been used there will be no need to give any further attention to the base of the job, but if it has been on a faceplate or screw chuck the screw holes can be plugged and the area polished. Green baize is not too good an idea, since it is certain to become soiled in time by scraps of butter or whatever.

for fit, and the area carefully enlarged if required. The tile is then set aside and the trough for the biscuits is turned, using the

14 Bandsaws

It is by no means necessary for anyone taking up woodturning to acquire a bandsaw immediately, but the value of these machines in a turner's shop is, in my view, so great that a chapter on the subject is justified. It is appreciated that many readers will have some degree of familiarity with bandsaws, but there will be plenty who have not used one, so I am not assuming any level of knowledge.

In essence, a bandsaw is a shape-cutting machine, but well-engineered versions, which are not the norm, will cut straight. One advantage over the circular saw where most home users are concerned, apart from the curve-cutting facility, is the fact that most machines produced for the domestic market have a depth of cut of about 6 inches. If one rules out stupidity on the part of the user, these machines are considerably safer in inexperienced hands than a circular saw. They are also extremely versatile.

The prospective buyer, in browsing through bandsaw advertisements in magazines, will soon come across the terms 'two-wheeler' and 'three-wheeler', which are to some extent self-explanatory. One has its blade passing over two wheels, the other three. The significance of this, however, is that bandsaws with three wheels have a larger 'throat' than the two-wheeled type, the throat being the dis-

tance between the blade and the 'column', which is the part of the bandsaw casing joining the upper and lower parts. The throat dimension will therefore indicate the amount of timber which can pass through this gap. It is not advisable to buy a bandsaw on the basis of this dimension unless there is some very good reason for so doing, since in most bandsaw operations the bulk of the wood passes on the other side of the blade. For most workers, depth of cut is more important than throat width. There are other points to be noted here, but before dealing with them I will give a general description of the bandsaw as such.

The name is derived from the fact that the blade is a flexible ribbon, or band, of steel, which is toothed all round one edge. This is carried on two or three rubber-tyred wheels, and facilities are provided for 'tracking' the blade so that it runs on the desired part of the wheel, and for moving one of the wheels in order to apply or release blade tension. The blade and wheels are contained within the bandsaw casing, parts of which can be removed for cleaning or when replacing blades.

There is a gap in the right-hand side of the casing, though in one or two machines this is on the left, where the table is fitted, this often being provided with a rip fence, the function of which I will explain in due course. There are also blade guides, and thrust rollers for the blade, which must be set exactly as recommended by the makers. The better machines have these guides and rollers both above and below the table, and I would not look twice at a bandsaw with only one set. Two sets of guides and rollers are essential to accuracy and trouble-free cutting, and well worth the little extra that they cost.

There are a few very small and relatively cheap bandsaws on the market, usually three-wheelers, but they do not qualify for inclusion here, being more or less toys as far as a woodturner is concerned. They should not be underestimated, however, by those engaged in toy making or the cutting of thin materials, as when used within their limits they are very useful. Our interest is in the larger machines, which will cut happily and efficiently through up to 6 inches of really hard timber without complaining or constantly breaking blades, which are not cheap. I have owned a total of eleven bandsaws over the years, and by far the best, though not the dearest, is one which I acquired a year or two ago. This is an Italian machine, manufactured by Lazari, under their Mini-Max label, and if kept in correct adjustment, its performance potential is remarkable. This machine is shown in the photographs, which will help to clarify my description of bandsaw construction. Having written several books and various magazine articles on the subject of woodworking machinery, I have to say that the bandsaw is one of the most difficult to write about, and can be among the more temperamental in use unless it is kept in correct adjustment.

The prospective purchaser of a bandsaw needs to be in possession of a fair amount of information if an expensive mistake is to be avoided. Some makes are best left alone, and these are not always the cheaper ones. It would be unfair for me to name them, since my views are to some extent subjective, but I will indicate the points to watch when selecting a bandsaw, which should be sufficient guide to help you make your choice.

Good blades are essential. They may cost more than bad ones, but their life will be far longer, and they will prove the more economical buy. There are two quite different kinds of blade material, one of which is silver in colour, the other dark blue. The silver variety has no place in my workshop, because I always begrudge time spent in fiddling with things which should not have gone wrong, and silver blades have inherent problems which I can well do without. The teeth of a bandsaw blade, like most other sawblades, have 'set', which with most saws provides a 'kerf' or sawcut which is a little wider than the blade, so preventing friction and overheating of the blade. This is true of bandsaw blades, but the kerf has another function, which is to allow the back of the blade to swing in the kerf when cutting curves, this being the principal function of the tool. An adequate degree of set is vital to satisfactory bandsaw performance, and one of the problems with silver blades is that if the teeth are allowed to run on the rubber tyres the downward-set teeth, those which point into the tyre, will lose their set and the blade will pull badly in one direction when cutting. The kerf will also become inadequate, the blade will tend to overheat and jam, and it is likely to 'bow' in the cut, producing a convex edge to the work. The edge of the job will also be burned in severe cases, and early blade breakage is almost certain. Some bandsaws, particularly the smaller three-wheelers, have to run with silver blades, because their wheels are small. This involves excessive flexing of the blade as it passes over the wheels, and metal fatigue will cause early breakage.

High-quality blue-steel bandsaw blades can be obtained from good suppliers, and are manufactured by firms like Milford, and Starret. These are a very different matter. They are made of stout gauge metal, thicker than the silver blades, and they are made in a manner which greatly increases their efficiency and longevity. The teeth are first cut and given the correct degree of set, then they are hardened, but the rest of the blade is left relatively soft. This means that the blade itself is still flexible while the teeth are hard enough to stand up to the hardest of woods, and the blade can be run on the tyres of the machine without loss of set. Anyone using a good blue-steel blade for the first time after experience with the silver ones will find that there really is no comparison.

Ready-made bandsaw blades are available, but I never use them. In the main they are badly made and have a self-destruct factor which I find quite unacceptable. The same thing applies to a fair extent to the blue blades, since one is at the mercy of the operator who cut and joined them, and they frequently break after having done very little work. It is well worth noting that if your machine is capable of using blue-steel blades, which will mean that it has a wheel diameter of about 10 inches upward, the process of making up your own blades is quick, easy, and saves a vast amount of money. I will describe the process before leaving this subject, but it may be best to finish the discussion of the bandsaw itself at this stage.

I am frequently asked whether investment in this type of machine is really worth while, and of course it is necessary to discuss the potential value of such a tool with the individual enquirer in the light of his or her current woodworking activities and of other factors. My experience has been that the vast majority of people who cannot quite see why they need a bandsaw will, if they acquire one, be wondering within a very short time how they ever managed without it. A good one cuts accurately and very fast, is quiet, and is far safer for beginners than other types of powered saw. Almost all the timber I cut for use in the lathe is sawn on the bandsaw. I use wood up to 5 or even 6 inches in thickness, and however hard, this is dealt with very rapidly. The curve-cutting capability is brought in when I have to cut discs of any size, from the vast numbers I cut for toy wheels, through various sizes of bowl, up to really large discs for special projects. Shaped parts for cabinet-making purposes, and legs for wine tables, are

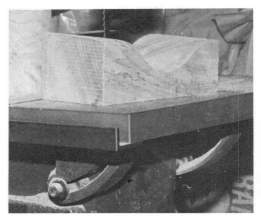

A good bandsaw will cut curves very rapidly in hard timber up to 6 inches thick.

other obvious jobs for this versatile machine. As I say, there is no need for one right at the start, though it would be nice to have, but the eventual purchase of a bandsaw should be the aim of any serious-minded beginner.

I will not take up space here with a detailed description of the correct setting up of these machines, stage by stage, as would be necessary in a book on machinery, but I must point out that if the best results are to be achieved, the setting must be carried out as recommended by the makers, and regularly checked. If a dust-extraction unit is not available, the machine must be stopped occasionally, its front covers removed, and the inside of the casing cleaned out. Special attention should be paid to the tyres, and particularly so when softwoods are being cut regularly, because lumps of resin building up on the rubber can cause blade breakage. A very common question from students who see me using the bandsaw in my workshop is 'what happens when the blade breaks?'. The answer is that nothing significant occurs. The blade is light, having little mass, and since the frictional drive of the rubber-tyred wheels is lost at the moment of breakage, the blade simply stops. There is usually a bit of a bang as it snaps, which may make the user jump, but that is all. If the blade has not done much work, those who make up their own can of course effect a repair quite easily, and the blade may then give long service.

The tables of bandsaws are normally provided with mechanisms which permit them to be tilted by up to 45 degrees, which is useful for those wishing to remove the corners of large squares before mounting them in the lathe. The removal of such corners on a bandsaw is less dangerous than with a circular saw, but

Ripping beech board on a Mini-Max bandsaw, using the rip fence. Note that the guard must be brought down close to the work.

unless the machine has a rip fence a piece of wood needs to be clamped to the table to support the material. Rip fences are quite useless on poor bandsaws, but will work well on good ones, and if a machine is demonstrated before purchase an example of this procedure should be requested. The rip fence is simply a rectangular sectioned piece of metal which can be clamped to the table, the wood running against it when being cut along its length.

Some machines have a slot in the table into which a mitre guide can be fitted, but the abysmal performance of many makes renders this idea almost useless. Good-quality saws, fitted with blue-steel blades which are in good condition will, however, work well with a mitre guide. This can be angled and set for the cutting of mitres

Tables of many bandsaws tilt to 45 degrees as here, but the rip fence should be used to support the timber.

One most important fact is that the wheels of the bandsaw should be of steel, not alloy. This gives them a flywheel effect, helping to prevent blade 'snatch', which is a frequent cause of premature blade failure. Steel wheels are usually finely balanced, and they make a tremendous difference to the sweet running of the machine.

The upper wheel of a Mini-Max bandsaw is large and heavy. Note the balancing holes near the top.

(45-degree angles) or for other angle-cutting requirements. When the guide has been set, and its runner placed in the table slot, the wood is held firmly against the mitre guide fence and pushed forward to the blade.

As with most other woodworking machines, the table should be of cast steel, not a light metal alloy, which is common. Steel remains flat and true, and will not be 'scuffed' and worn by the hard timbers. There is an insert at the centre of the table, sometimes made of metal, but more commonly of wood, which closely surrounds the blade to support very thin material. If of wood these can easily be replaced, when necessary, by the owner.

As I remarked earlier, there should be a set of guides and thrust rollers both above and below the table. These must be set with care, or the performance of the tool will be poor. When the blade begins to cut it is pushed backwards by the wood,

A typical guide and roller assembly which should be provided both above and below the table of the bandsaw. Note the thrust roller behind the blade, and the wooden adjustable guides.

so the thrust rollers, which are small bearings, are set to clear the blade by a tiny amount when it is stationary. The guides are on either side of the blade, almost, but not quite, making contact with it. They prevent any undesirable twisting of the blade when cutting, and are of great importance. They may be made of wood, a soft metal alloy such as phosphor bronze, or of plastic, but most bandsawyers cut a supply of their own from the densest hardwood they can find, and these will work as well as any.

There are one or two points regarding the setting of bandsaws which are worth noting, one of which relates to the amount of tension applied to the blade. There is an adjuster for this, which on my own machine is sensibly in the form of a recessed Allen screw, beyond the reach of compulsive knob-twiddlers. There are no firm rules about tension, but the maker's instructions should be followed as far as possible. Some people advise the removal of tension from the blade at the end of the

day, and its reinstatement when the saw is next used, but this should be avoided since alterations to the tension tend to disturb other settings. I have never followed the practice, nor found it to be necessary. It is also occasionally suggested that blades should always be tracked by means of the tracking control so that their teeth project over the edge of the tyre. This is not always practicable, however, since blades can be obtained in widths down to as little as $\frac{1}{8}$ inch. I have always run my blades on the tyre, and found no ill-effects.

Finally, just a few brief notes on cutting, with a mention of the wide range of blades which is available for bandsaws. Those requiring very smooth edge finishes, which I normally do not, will use blades with a large number of teeth. If the requirement is for rapid cutting and efficient waste removal from the gullets of the blade, 'skip tooth' blades will be employed. These, effectively, have alternate teeth missed out altogether, giving wide curved gullets which will eject waste even from damp timber. In general I use a 3-TPI (teeth per inch) skip tooth blade, and I find that a blade width of $\frac{3}{8}$ inch copes well with most of my work.

Having said that blades can easily be made up by the user, I will describe the process, but there is little to it, and the making of a new blade takes me less than five minutes. Those making their own blades will buy the blade material in lengths of 100 feet, contained in special packs from which the required length can be withdrawn. *Never* open one of these packs, because the blade will fly all over the place and may cause injury. Blades can only be made successfully from blue steel, which is of a sufficiently heavy gauge to provide a strong joint.

The required length is cut from the roll, the measurement being taken from another blade, and the ends of this length are ground at a slight angle to produce a 'scarf' or bevel. This takes a few moments only, but make sure that the bevels are ground so that they complement each other, and will meet correctly. This done, the ground areas, which should not be touched with the fingers, are 'tinned' with silver solder, using a butane torch and the requisite flux (which is borax). The blade is now set up in a small jig, which can be obtained from specialist woodworking suppliers and which will ensure that the back edges of the two ends are correctly aligned. The ends are positioned so that they overlap each other by precisely the required amount, the flame is applied until the solder is seen to 'flow', and the joint is then gripped with a pair of pliers as the flame is withdrawn. It is as simple as that, but *do* ensure that the blade is not overheated. It should not pass the 'cherry red' stage, and if you feel that it may have done so, allow it to cool and then heat it again to cherry red and allow it to cool slowly. The job can then be done over again. All that remains is to file or grind away any excess solder, and the blade should provide good service.

In order to avoid expensive wastage of material, it is advisable to cut a few short lengths of blade and practise on these before making any proper blades, but there is little to the process and it will pay handsomely.

15 Copy Turning

It is unfortunately true that many people fail to become woodturners in the full sense, but end up as whittlers or doodlers in that they make 'one-off' shapes, and polish them when they feel that the shape will do. This is fun, but a prime requirement for a woodturner is to be able to take on any job which can be done on a lathe if it is offered, and most of this is awkward stuff which the ubiquitous 'chap down the road' would not look at. Inability to copy successfully rules out furniture work, which is a very interesting area – chairs with one leg are a bit unstable. Those wishing to make some money from the craft will soon find that repetition work is an excellent source of profit if it can be done efficiently and accurately in a reasonable time.

At this stage I must point out that the key to success is constant practice, which trains the eye and the hand to work in unison. Without this practice there can be little hope of progress. I am often asked what devices are obtainable for copy turning, and whether there is anything which will make it easy. There are commercial machines which will copy virtually anything at a ridiculous speed, but they cost ridiculous sums of money, and are not within our parameters. There are also some little aids which have various degrees of value, and I will discuss these,

but first it is important to understand what is meant by a 'copying attachment' for a lathe. These are becoming more common, and they have their uses. They also have certain drawbacks and limitations, and since they can cost more than the lathe itself, a prospective purchaser needs to be wary of them. Prices of copying attachments vary widely: some are relatively cheap while others will make the piggy bank emit a very hollow sound when tapped. They all operate in much the same way, but some are better designed and engineered than others.

Taking the copying attachment which is available for the Mini-Max lathe as an example, this is a large and heavy device which attaches to the rear of the machine. It is complicated, but I will try to make the explanation as clear as I can. The copying process relies upon the use of a template, made by the user, which fits into the copier. These templates can be made from hard timber, plywood or even good-quality hardboard, but in most cases I prefer to turn an example of the object I wish to produce, making it about $\frac{1}{8}$ inch larger in diameter than the required finished dimension. I then take a slice out of this turning, on the bandsaw, cutting about $\frac{1}{8}$ inch each side of centre along the length of the wood, so producing a flat, double-sided template. Note that these copiers cannot deal with detail, only with straight surfaces or flowing curves. The shape of the cutter precludes any possibility of producing beads, V-cuts, or sharp changes of angle. Such detail is left out of the template and must be put in by hand later.

The template is fixed into its holder in the copier, and the profile-follower, which is a cylindrical pin, is set to rest against its largest diameter. It is better to have the blank ready turned to a cylinder a fraction larger than required, since although it is possible to rough down from a square on the copier, the process is very time-consuming. There are two controls on the copier, one being a handwheel which moves the profile-follower along the template and the cutter along the blank, the other being a small control by means of which the cutter can be fed into the wood a little more after each traverse. It may sound complex, but it is very simple in practice, and the copier can be operated by a totally unskilled person, which is one of its advantages.

The cutter can operate when moving in either direction, so at the end of each traverse it is fed into the wood a little, and the profile-follower contacts more of the template at each pass. There is no possibility of overcutting, which means the removal of too much material, and some people find this performance fascinating to watch. One problem is that the cutters are never anything like as efficient as a properly applied chisel or gouge, since they must of necessity cut across the grain and have no slicing action. The results therefore tend to be rough, and on pine they are definitely shaggy. The cutter is usually a small cup- or gouge-shaped object, which takes quite a beating and requires frequent attention to produce the best results. It cannot be ground as the normal turning

tools would be, but has to be sharpened with small oilstones and extreme care. On some dense hardwoods it will do a reasonable job, but there will be few occasions when subsequent abrasive work is not imperative.

By now the whole business may be starting to sound like a waste of time and timber, but this is not so. In certain applications these copiers are worth buying, but I would emphasise that they are not suitable for hobby use, where the intension is to produce the odd set of table legs, or pair of lamps. They are of real use only to those who have occasion to make large quantities of items for sale, such as balusters for staircases, furniture legs, or similar products.

The great advantage offered in such situations is the saving of the time of the skilled turner. He or she can employ an unskilled worker, who has to know no more than how to put the blanks in the lathe, and how to turn the handles of the copier. Large quantities of objects can be produced like this, and the skilled worker can subsequently pop the rough copy into a lathe, clean up all surfaces with a sharp gouge or chisel, and insert any beads or other detail work. There is no necessity for any measuring. The workpiece is slightly oversize, and if the turner skims $\frac{1}{16}$ inch from it, the job is done.

It is appreciated that this is not a full and thorough exploration of copiers, but it should serve to show their merits and demerits, and hopefully will save some hobbyists from disappointment which would be inevitable if such a device were purchased without the benefit of a really thorough demonstration.

Numerous proprietary gadgets are advertised to assist the frustrated woodturner and to make life easier, but most do nothing of the kind. Some thought will reveal that they merely serve to indicate, after the wood has been cut, where things have gone wrong, and by that time it is a little late. We are blessed with the power of judgement, or most of us are, and this judgement should be trained and applied, with as much practice as possible. Even so, despair is not called for. There are one or two approaches which I have found over the years to be really helpful.

One simple aid which I tend to use a good deal is a flap of plywood hinged to the bench at the back of the lathe, which can be raised to a vertical position by pulling a string which passes through a convenient hook above the machine. To this plywood flap the turner can attach either the pattern from which the shape is being copied, or a drawing. The method of using this equipment is to raise the flap and sight across the work in the lathe to make comparisons. With a little practice it becomes very easy to see exactly where more wood needs to be removed, and indeed where too much has been cut already. The old saying about more haste and less speed is very appropriate in copy-turning, which should never be hurried.

Those who feel that they may want to undertake a fair amount of copy work could do worse than to take advantage of a very old idea which works quite well. This involves the use of what is known as a 'semaphore jig', which is one of the numerous old ideas which people keep 'inventing' and sending in to bored magazine editors. It can be constructed in the home workshop in well under a day by a competent woodworker, and if made with care will be both a useful adjunct to copy-turning and an interesting object with which to impress visitors.

The system relies upon a number of

'Semaphore' jig for turning wheels. The flag is set to touch the master wheel, but drops.

The blank replaces the master and turning continues until the flag drops. My wife likes this job, as the photograph shows!

The flag drops. Production of identical-diameter wheels by this method is simple.

little 'flags', which fall when the work has been turned to a certain diameter. It is ingenious, and children will watch it with great interest.

The first part of the construction looks rather like a towel rail, in that there is a base board which has two triangular pieces of wood at right-angles to it, one at each end. These are drilled to take a length of 1-inch dowel, which can be purchased locally by those who don't fancy turning it. I use blockboard for the bases of these things, and for the end pieces, making these to a size which will bring the dowel up roughly level with the lathe centres. The exact size required for the rest of the components can be worked out according to the lathe in use, and these consist of a multitude of small pieces of wood, about ¼ inch thick. These have rounded ends and are drilled to fit neatly over the dowel. They are then cut through at one end and drilled so that a bolt and wing nut can be fitted, allowing them to be adjusted on the dowel and clamped in place. The other end of these pieces is slotted with a saw to accept small flags which have rounded ends. The flags and the pieces into which they fit are drilled to take small bolts, and the flags must be free-swinging in their holders. It is in fact preferable to make the flags from metal which is fairly heavy; wooden ones tend to bounce too much in the early stages of a turning, but they will do at a pinch. The method of using this device becomes quite clear as soon as a job is set up in the lathe, and I find the system very helpful.

The idea is to mount the leg or baluster which is to be copied between centres, and then to set all the flags, or as many as are felt necessary, so that they just touch the selected diameters of the job, but will fall. The pattern is then removed from the lathe, and a piece of wood is turned down to a fraction more than its required maximum diameter. The flags are now laid on the wood, and there are two courses open to the turner. Either the work can be turned just far enough for the flags to fall, or a thin parting tool can be taken in opposite each flag until it falls, the resulting slots being used as depth guides. Both systems work well, it is a matter of personal preference. The value of this approach lies in the fact that it allows the turner to concentrate on the shaping, while the flags control the diameters, so saving a lot of time which would otherwise be spent in measuring and calipering the job.

I think I have tried most of the other oddities which have appeared from time to time, but the two I have described here seem to me to be the only really useful types.

It is my earnest hope that this book will help those who are struggling to learn the techniques of this absorbing craft, and that it will inspire others who have not yet taken up a gouge or a chisel to use on a lathe. The pleasure to be derived from creative hobbies is enormous, and the sense of achievement when a job goes well is a joy to the heart.

Index